MEL BAY PRESENTS

GREENWICH VILLAGE

The Happy Folk Singing Days
1950s and 1960s

with Musical Notation,
Guitar Chords and Arrangements
for Mountain Dulcimer

by Ralph Lee Smith with Madeline MacNeil

1 2 3 4 5 6 7 8 9 0

© 2008 BY MEL BAY PUBLICATIONS, INC., PACIFIC, MO 63069.
ALL RIGHTS RESERVED. INTERNATIONAL COPYRIGHT SECURED. B.M.I. MADE AND PRINTED IN U.S.A.
No part of this publication may be reproduced in whole or in part, stored in a retrieval system, or transmitted in any form
or by any means, electronic, mechanical, photocopy, recording, or otherwise, without written permission of the publisher.

Visit us on the Web at www.melbay.com — E-mail us at email@melbay.com

CONTENTS

LITTLE STREET, HAPPY DAYS 7
    21 Jones Street
    4 Jones Street

FOLK SINGING IN WASHINGTON SQUARE 9
    An Unhappy Parks Department

THE VILLAGE COFFEEHOUSES 13

THE FOLKLORE CENTER 17

ALLAN BLOCK'S SANDAL SHOP 21

HAPPY SUMMER DAYS 23

THE DULCIMER IN GREENWICH VILLAGE..25
    Jean Ritchie, Princess of the Dulcimer
    Three Village Dulcimers

THE LITTLE RECORD COMPANIES 29

THE SANDAL SHOP MUSIC PRESERVED 30

LET'S SING AND PLAY AGAIN! 31

VILLAGE SCRAPBOOK 32

WELL, FOR GOSH SAKES!
THEY'RE BACK IN WASHINGTON SQUARE! 39

POSTSCRIPT: "A TIME OF JOY FROM OUR YOUTH,"
    by Eric Nagler, 60s Village Banjo Player 95

~~~~~~

Title page photo: five friends singing in a concert at the Folklore Center in Greenwich Village, May 22, 1967.
Left to right John Burke, Kenny Kosek, Andy May, Richard Blaustein, and Ralph: A flyer for the concert appears on page 33.
Photo by Jack Prelutsky. Used with permission.

Cover drawing of Washington Square Arch and the Washington Square Park fountain by Barbara Seymour.
The four charming drawings in the Songs section are also by Barbara. Used with permission.

~~~~~~

My First Dulcimer

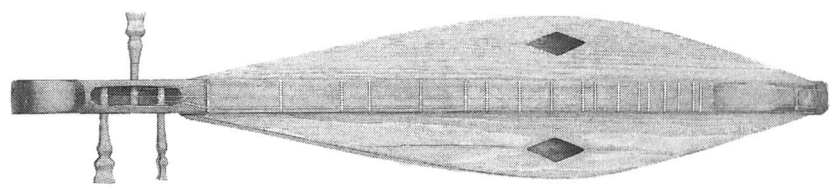

Purchased at the Folklore Center in Greenwich Village, c. 1958.
A beautiful North Carolina folk creation. See Page 27

SONGS AND DULCIMER TUNINGS

Charley's Neat (DAG) 41
Finger Ring (DAA) 42
Finger Ring (DAD) 43
Dance All Night With a Bottle in Your Hand (DAA) 44
Way Down Town (DAA) 47
Way Down Town (DAD) 49
Johnson Boys (DAA) 50
Johnson Boys (DAD) 52
The Dying Ranger (DGD) 54
Little Moses (DAA) 56
Little Moses (DAD) 58
Run Mountain (DAA) 59
Run Mountain (DAD) 61
Roll In My Sweet Baby's Arms (DAA) 62
Roll In My Sweet Baby's Arms (DAD) 63
Single Girl, Married Girl (DAA) 64
Single Girl, Married Girl (DAD) 66
Chickens Are a-Crowin' (DAG) 67
The Brave Engineer (DAA) 68
The Brave Engineer (DAD) 70
Ain't That Skippin' And a-Flyin' (DAA) 72
Ain't That Skippin' And a-Flyin' (DAD) 73
East Virginia (DAA) 74
East Virginia (DAD) 75
Pretty Little Turtle Dove (DAA) 76
Pretty Little Turtle Dove (DAD) 78
Hop High Ladies (DAA) 79
Hop High Ladies (DAD) 81
Goin' Across the Sea (DAA) 82
Roll On The Ground (DAA) 84
Roll On The Ground (DAD) 85
Likes Likker Better Than Me (DAA) 86
Likes Likker Better Than Me (DAD) 88
Georgia Railroad (DAA) 89
Georgia Railroad (DAD) 91
Who's Going To Shoe Your Pretty Little Foot? (DAA) 92
Who's Going To Shoe Your Pretty Little Foot? (DAD) 94

Greenwich Village Map

1. Washington Square Park. Hub and symbol of the Village.
2. MacDougal Street, below Washington Square Park, between West 3rd Street and Bleeker Street. This was "Coffeehouse Row."
3. Jones Street. Ralph lived on this one-block street from 1957 to 1971.
4. Allan Block's Sandal Shop, 171 West 4th Street. A major venue for Old Time Music.
5. Joe's Restaurant, corner of Jones and West 4th Street, where folkies ate "on the tab."
6. The Folklore Center, location No. 1, 110 MacDougal Street, c. 1957-1963.
7. The Folklore Center, location No. 2, 321 Sixth Avenue, c. 1964-1973.
8. Circle-in-the-Square Theater, on Sheridan Square, where Ralph heard Jean Ritchie perform.
9. Pete Seeger's apartment, 119 MacDougal Street, where Allan Block slept on Pete's floor.
10. Alan Lomax's apartment, 121 W. 3rd Street. Ralph Rinzler, founder of the Smithsonian's Folklife Festival on the Mall in Washington, also lived here.
11. Jean Ritchie and George Pickow's apartment, 88 7th Avenue South.
12. First office of Elektra Records, 361 Bleeker Street.
13. Office of Tradition Records, 131 Christopher Street.
14. Shop of Peter Carbone, instrument maker and restorer, 184 Bleeker Street.

"Positively 4th Street"

This photo was taken by *New York Times* photographer Joyce Dopkeen, to illustrate an article in the June 29, 2003 issue, entitled, "Still Positively 4th Street," after Bob Dylan's well-known song. The photo shows the intersection of Jones Street and West 4th Street, a folk music crossroads in the 60s.

X marks the spot where, in the winter of 1962-63, the picture of Bob and his companion, Susan Rotolo, was taken for the cover of Bob's breakthrough album, *The Freewheelin' Bob Dylan*. Songs on the album included "Blowin' in the Wind."

No. 4 Jones Street, where Ralph lived, was just to the left of the photo's left-hand margin. Allan Block's Sandal Shop, at 171 West 4th Street, was just to the left of the photographer, who was standing on an adjoining stoop. Bob's first New York apartment, which he rented after sleeping on friends' chairs and couches for about a year, was at 161 West 4th Street, a few doors down from the Sandal Shop.

"The entrance to Joe's Restaurant, where folk singers ate on the tab, is on the corner, facing both streets. It is long gone, and a much fancier place has moved in. In case you are puzzled, the "person" sitting atop the awning over the restaurant entrance is a mannequin!

Bob Dylan was here.

No. 21 Jones Street.
A relic of old Greenwich Village. Since this picture was taken, the gray paint has been removed from the rest of the brick.

No. 4 Jones Street.
Ralph's apartment, No. 6, was on the left, two floors up from the awning. Bob Dylan and Susan Rotolo had their picture taken for his second album, The Freewheelin' Bob Dylan, *just to the right of the parked car.*

A corner of Ralph's apartment at 4 Jones Street, 1969.
Hanging on the left is an early McSpadden dulcimer. Hanging on the right is Ralph's first dulcimer, purchased at the Folklore Center in the late 1950s. Standing on the floor is Ralph's Jean Ritchie dulcimer, purchased at the Folklore Center ten years later (for both dulcimers, see page 27). To the left are a 1957 Martin D-18 guitar and an 1890 Cole banjo, the latter purchased by Ralph at the Folklore Center about 1960. The banjo appears on the cover of the album, Ralph Lee Smith and Allan Block, Meadowlands MS-1, 1971. In 2002, Ralph sold the banjo to Lea Coryell of Herndon, Virginia, a traditional banjo player and enthusiast, who had it fully restored and uses it for performances and demonstrations. Photo by Carol Goodden. Used with permission.

LITTLE STREET, HAPPY DAYS

In 1957, I moved into a tiny apartment on Jones Street, a little one-block street in the heart of Greenwich Village. My timing was very lucky. The Folk Revival was poised to take off, with Greenwich Village as its national and world crossroads.

In Washington Square, ever-larger crowds gathered on Sunday afternoons, to sing, play, and listen to folk music. In that year, down on MacDougal Street, a little establishment called The Folklore Center opened its doors. Almost immediately, it became a national and even world hub for the emerging folk music movement. A few months later, the first of the now-legendary folk-singing coffeehouses opened, just off MacDougal Street. And right outside my window, Allan Block's Sandal Shop was becoming a gathering place for people who were rediscovering old-time mountain music and were teaching themselves to play it.

I played dulcimer and harmonica in the Village, in the old-time mountain music part of the scene, in the late 1950s and through the 60s. I didn't become famous and I didn't become rich, but I had a good time! This book describes some of this vanished world, and some of the songs and tunes that we learned and played.

21 JONES STREET

From 1957 to 1964, I lived at 21 Jones Street, which is a dilapidated but delightful survivor of the old Village. It consists of two small, four-story brick buildings, front and rear, both with skylights for one of the top apartments, separated by a little courtyard with a dusty, leaf-clogged fountain that no longer worked. The right-hand side of the front building appears to have been built over an alleyway. One entered at street level, below the addition, walked through a brick-paved passageway, and entered and crossed a small courtyard to the entrance to the rear building. There were two postage-stamp-sized one-room apartments on each floor. I lived in Apartment 6 on the third floor of the rear building. The rent was $78 per month.

4 JONES STREET

In 1964, I moved a few yards up and across the street to a three-room apartment at 4 Jones Street. The building was very old, probably mid-19th Century. As with 21 Jones Street, there were two apartments on each floor, and by coincidence, I again had Apartment 6 on the third floor. It was a railroad flat, with the bedroom sandwiched in between the living room and kitchen. There were beautiful, wide pine floorboards, and fireplaces in both living room and kitchen, of which the one in the living room worked excellently. The rent was $126 per month, and later went up to $140.

In 1995, 4 Jones Street was demolished to make way for a low-rise apartment building. In 2007, a luxury one-room apartment in the new building, with a balcony but no fireplace, was offered on the Internet for $3995 a month. Yes, you read it right.

A Crowd in Washington Square Enjoys a Group of Folk Singers.
The players on the right include a washtub bass player, and a guitar player who is really belting those verses out. The peg heads of one and perhaps two additional instruments are visible, lower right. This slightly fuzzy photo is an enlargement from a 35mm contact strip that was supplied to Ralph by the late Lee Hoffman. If either the prints or negatives survived, Lee did not know their whereabouts. In the late 1950s, Lee founded and edited a small folk music magazine called Caravan. The contact strip is probably from Caravan's files. The photos were taken by Aaron Rennert of Photo-Sound Associates. Photo by Photo-Sound Associates. Used with permission.

Bluegrass and Old Timey Medley
The players are: Bluegrass banjo player Roger Sprung, and old-timey players John Cohen, guitar, and Mike Seeger, mandolin. Note the crowd surrounding another singing and playing group across the fountain. Photo by Photo-Sound Associates. Used with permission.

Mighty Concentration
That's teenager Winnie Winston bent over his guitar, while an unknown Helpful Harry taps out a rhythm on the guitar's body. Luke Faust, on banjo, looks unflappable. Luke and Winnie both became distinguished performers, with Winnie specializing in bluegrass banjo and pedal steel. Ralph and Winnie both played on the Elektra record, Old Time Banjo Project, released in 1964. Photo by Andrew Alpern. Used with permission.

FOLK SINGING IN WASHINGTON SQUARE

"That Washington Square Sunday afternoon scene was a great catalyst for my whole generation," Dave Van Ronk, a top Village coffeehouse singer of the 60s, wrote in his book, *The Mayor of MacDougal Street*. "It kept getting bigger and bigger every year, and by the late 1950s it had become a tourist attraction as well."

Folk singing began in Washington Square just after World War II, and became increasingly popular in the 1950s. Folksingers gathered in Washington Square Park from 1:00 to 6:00 p.m. on Sunday afternoons, which was the time specified by the official permit issued by the Department of Parks and Recreation. The folk singers brought guitars, banjos, and other instruments, and joined with friends and others to sing and play. Groups of several players would get together around or near the fountain in the center of the park, play, and swap songs, surrounded by other players picking away on the fringes, and by happy listeners.

In the earlier years, participants included, not only folk singing groups, but also international dancing groups, and solo instrumentalists and vocalists. Folk songs included standard fare from such sources as Burl Ives records and *The Fireside Book of Folk Songs*. In his book, *New York in the Fifties*, writer Dan Wakefield describes the Square as a place "where we used to go on Sundays to hear the folk singers and mingle with the crowd, which always included people we knew. It was a community scene, like people in a small town gathering for a concert, but instead of a brass band we had guitar players, and we sang along with them, telling Michael to row the boat ashore or proclaiming this land is your land, this land is my land."

The scene grew in both size and repertoire. Standard fare on any 60s weekend included a considerable number of banjo and fiddle tunes from the Southern Appalachian tradition, which someone had learned some time ago and which the players then learned from each other. Many of the singers and players were launched into an additional voyage of discovery – bluegrass. The bluegrass repertoire and the traditional repertoire substantially overlapped but were not full duplicates, and the banjo-playing techniques were different. Banjo player Roger Sprung almost single-handedly introduced Southern bluegrass music to New York through his playing in Washington Square.

Smooth Coordination
Bob Yellin gets off a smooth run on banjo, backed by reliable Dave Sternlight on guitar. Note heavily packed crowd. Photo by Photo-Sound Associates. Used with permission.

AN UNHAPPY PARKS DEPARTMENT

When the Department of Parks and Recreation permit for Sunday afternoon folk singing came up for renewal in 1961, efforts were made to block it. Opposition was centered in the ethnic Italian community just south of Washington Square, where many residents were unhappy about the growing presence in their neighborhood of young, upper-middle class "hippies" and "beatniks" who apparently didn't have to work, and who seemed to be overrunning their world. The permit was not renewed. When police attempted to quell a protest in the park, there was a confrontation and scuffle. It was delicious stuff for the New York tabloids. "3000 BEATNIKS RIOT IN VILLAGE," the *New York Mirror* proclaimed.

Page 1 headline of the New York Mirror, *April 10, 1961, reporting on the scuffle between folk singers and police in Washington Square the preceding day. Courtesy Israel Young.*

"Right to Sing" rallies were promptly organized, and were attended by large, peaceful crowds. On a quieter but highly effective level, many Village residents, including persons living along the Park who would be adversely affected by the scene if anybody was, came to the singers' aid and defense. If the kids had no influence at City Hall, many of these people did.

In addition, it was the old story of the enemy turning out to be us. In addition to folk singers such as beautiful Maria d'Amato (later Maria Muldaur), born and raised in the Italian community south of Washington Square, there was an Italian garage mechanic who loved to come to the Park on Sunday afternoons to play his mandolin and sing. When he refused to leave, the fuzz arrested him. This was not what the opponents of singing in the park had intended to achieve.

An embarrassed and defeated Parks Department entered into negotiations that resulted in renewal of the permit, and Sunday afternoon folk singing in Washington Square was joyously launched again. It continued through the 60s.

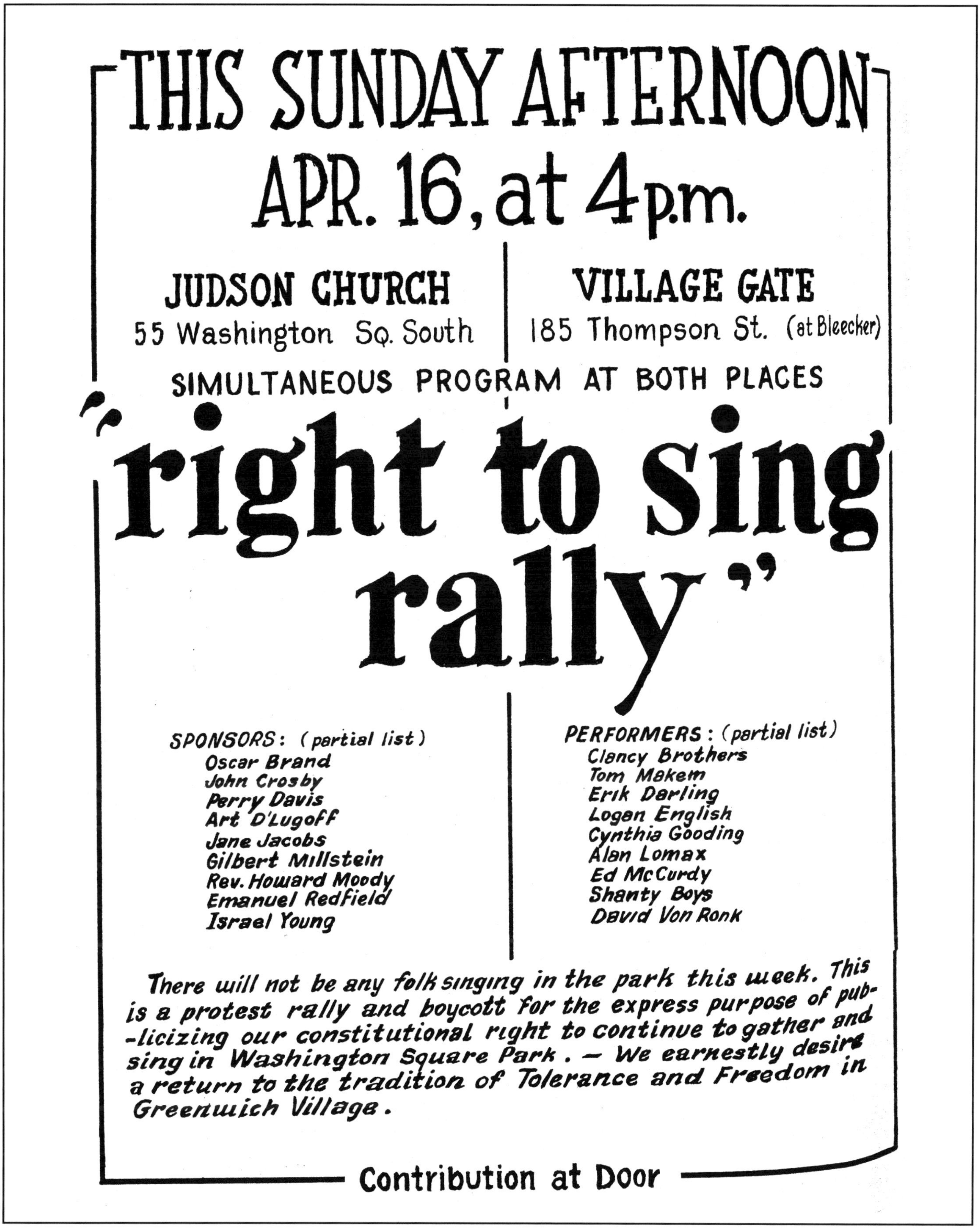

THIS SUNDAY AFTERNOON APR. 16, at 4 p.m.

JUDSON CHURCH	VILLAGE GATE
55 Washington Sq. South	185 Thompson St. (at Bleecker)

SIMULTANEOUS PROGRAM AT BOTH PLACES

"right to sing rally"

SPONSORS: (partial list)
- Oscar Brand
- John Crosby
- Perry Davis
- Art D'Lugoff
- Jane Jacobs
- Gilbert Millstein
- Rev. Howard Moody
- Emanuel Redfield
- Israel Young

PERFORMERS: (partial list)
- Clancy Brothers
- Tom Makem
- Erik Darling
- Logan English
- Cynthia Gooding
- Alan Lomax
- Ed McCurdy
- Shanty Boys
- David Von Ronk

There will not be any folk singing in the park this week. This is a protest rally and boycott for the express purpose of publicizing our constitutional right to continue to gather and sing in Washington Square Park. — We earnestly desire a return to the tradition of Tolerance and Freedom in Greenwich Village.

— Contribution at Door —

Flyer for Protest Rally

After the confrontation between police and folk singers, rallies and demonstrations were promptly organized to protest the City Hall ban on folk singing in the Park. Note from the date of the New York Mirror *headline that this one occurred just a week after the scuffle in Washington Square. Courtesy Israel Young.*

The Figaro Coffeehouse
One of the first of the "new style" coffeehouses, at the corner of MacDougal and Bleeker Streets, in an early 60s photograph. Today, it has a fancier sign and much, much fancier prices. Photo by Robert Otter. Used with permission of Ned Otter.

Old-style Espresso in the Gaslight Coffeehouse
An attractive young lady operates an old-style espresso machine in the Gaslight Coffeehouse, 1959. Throughout the 60s, most Village coffeehouses had these large, traditional machines rather than the newer machines, familiar to patrons of today's Starbucks, which were just coming into use. Photo by United Press International. Used with permission.

1959 - Village Coffeehouse
A busy scene in a Village coffeehouse, 1959. Two things are worth noting: five of the seven patrons sitting at the two front tables are smoking, and the patrons include at least two black persons. By the time the civil rights revolution came to America in the 60s, Village business establishments had been welcoming blacks for decades. Ralph cannot remember which coffeehouse is shown here. Can any reader help? New York Daily News photo. Used with permission.

THE VILLAGE COFFEEHOUSES

While folk singing flourished in Washington Square, a coffeehouse scene emerged along MacDougal Street, directly to the South. Several small coffeehouses already existed there, which were culturally a part of the old Italian community. In the early 50s, the Rienzi coffeehouse opened. It was the first MacDougal Street coffeehouse that was not closely tied to the Italian community, and whose clientele consisted principally of bohemians, middle-class residents from other parts of the Village, high school and college students, and tourists. The Rienzi offered poetry readings, art exhibits, and tables for playing chess. In 1956, the Figaro opened in good-sized premises at the intersection of MacDougal and Bleeker Streets. The Rienzi is gone but the Figaro is still there, and is a Village landmark.

The first Greenwich Village coffeehouse to feature folk singing was the Café Bizarre, which was opened by Rick Allmen on West 3rd Street, just off MacDougal, in 1957. The Bizarre was an instant success, and soon there were folk singing coffeehouses all up, down and near MacDougal Street. Leading venues included the Café Wha?, the Gaslight, the Caricature, the Commons, the Fat Black Pussycat, the Bitter End, the Village Gate, and Gerde's Folk City, which was technically a bar rather than a coffeehouse.

Some of the coffeehouses were "basket houses," in which unpaid performers did their best and passed the basket. Some, like the Wha? and the Gaslight, held what we now call open mikes during the afternoon, and presented paid – modestly paid! – performers of more proven abilities, in the evening. "Proof" often consisted of having issued one or more recordings.

The coffeehouses made an important contribution to the Folk Revival by offering venues in which one could perform before a genuine sit-down audience, and not necessarily a friendly one. In the coffeehouses, eager aspirants could and did learn the requirements of professional entertainment – or learned that they didn't have it and couldn't achieve it. Describing The Gaslight in his book, *Chronicles*, Bob Dylan put it all in one sentence: "It was a real stage with a real audience, and it was where the real action was."

The coffeehouses fostered the advent of a new kind of musician in America – the singer-songwriter. Singer-songwriters who emerged from the Village coffeehouse scene included Dylan, Tom Paxton, and Phil Ochs. Increasingly, many "folk singers" in the coffeehouses sang songs of recent or current composition, rather than traditional songs.

The repertoire of the coffeehouse singers favored appealing, audience-friendly material, a personal style, and skillful performance. Sources of the singers' material included books, and recordings by the big new folk stars such as Joan Baez and the Clancy Brothers. In 1966, Oak Publications published *The Coffeehouse Songbook*, offset directly from a typescript, with handwritten musical notation, and transcribed directly from coffeehouse singing throughout the U.S. It is a marvelous document of its times.

HIGH TIDE: MACDOUGAL

MacDougal Street - East side
The east side of MacDougal Street, a block below Washington Square, looking downtown. The Kettle of Fish Bar was a favorite of both folk singers and the Beat poets and writers. The Folklore Center's quatrefoil sign is in the far distance. The Street was honeycombed with little basements, half-below street level, such as the one in the foreground. The coffeehouses rented these little spaces and moved in. The Gaslight, at 116 MacDougal Street, a couple of doors closer to the camera than the Folklore Center, famous for its hosting of Bob Dylan, occupied a former coal cellar. Photo by Robert Otter. Used with permission of Ned Otter.

MacDougal Street - West side
The west side of MacDougal Street, looking uptown. Past the Minetta Tavern is the Café Wha?, boldly advertising its free hootenanny. Photo by Robert Otter. Used with permission of Ned Otter.

Café Why Not?
The Café Why Not?, a typical "basket house," set up in one of MacDougal Street's half-below-street-level basements. Photo by Mike Nogami. Used with permission.

STREET IN THE 1960s

Fat Black Pussycat
The rear of the Fat Black Pussycat, on Minetta Street. The front entrance was on MacDougal Street. The Pussycat was originally called the Commons. Both were folk singing venues. Both are gone, but the Pussycat's painted sign, a rare survival, can still be seen.

Summer night on MacDougal Street
MacDougal Street on a summer night, with crowds overflowing the sidewalk and onto the street. These crowds became so large that, for awhile, the police put up barricades on weekend evenings to prevent cars from entering the "folk singing block." The big crowds translated into business for the coffeehouses, and full baskets in the basket houses! Photo by Robert Otter. Used with permission of Ned Otter.

Movie scenes
In this photo, bystanders are watching a movie scene being shot in front of the Café Wha? In the 60s, the Village in general and MacDougal Street in particular, were favorite places for shooting movie scenes. Photo by Mike Nogami. Used with permission.

Folklore Center jamming
Allan Block and Ralph jamming in the Folklore Center, c. 1964. Ralph is playing his Frank Glenn dulcimer. The flyer partially obscured by Ralph's head advertises a concert by the traditional banjo player Dock Boggs, brought to New York by the Friends of Old Time Music. Above it is a sign reading, "No Bluegrass Bands on Sundays." Sundays were for old-time music only. Photographer unknown.

Folklore Center
The Folklore Center, 110 MacDougal Street. From this tiny premises, a musical revolution radiated out to the Village, to America and to the world. Israel (Izzy) Young, founder and proprietor, can be seen in the window, on the left, with a friend or customer on the right. Photo by Robert Otter. Used with permission of Ned Otter.

Opening Day
Folk singers and well-wishers gather at the Folklore Center on its opening day in April 1957. They include: Roy Berkeley, in white shirt; Cynthia Gooding, on his left; Una Ritchie, Jean Ritchie's sister, in the doorway; Jean Ritchie, with dulcimer; Happy Traum, next to Jean; Molly Scott, next to Happy. Photo by George Pickow. Used with permission.

THE FOLKLORE CENTER

In April 1957, a 29-year-old bookseller named Israel Young took a lease on a little storefront at 110 MacDougal Street, called it The Folklore Center, and installed a selection of new and used books on folklore and folk music, and a few bins of records. He had intended simply to open a book-and-record store, but instead he became a central figure in the Folk Revival.

Almost immediately, the Folklore Center became the informal headquarters of the Greenwich Village folk scene, both for folk singers in the Village and for those arriving from out of town. Bob Dylan even wrote a song called "The Talking Folklore Center." Izzy also sponsored concerts that were held in the store.

"I opened my store," Izzy told a conference on the Folk Revival at Indiana University in 1991, "and in weeks I'm a world-famous personality. I get a call from Al Grossman [who became Bob Dylan's agent, and who created the folk singing group Peter, Paul and Mary] in Chicago, that Peggy Seeger is passing through and can I do a concert for her? So that's how I started my concert series. Jack Elliott was coming back from Europe, so I had a concert for him. And Alan Lomax was coming back from Europe, so I had a concert with him. I made a party for him in my store as well as for a woman I was in love with who had just returned from Israel, and they left the party together." Poor Izzy!

"The artists and I shared the gate equally," Izzy continued. "I never had to sign a contract. It turned out that I was paying people more than folk singers were getting paid at the famous basket houses, and everyone understood that people at my concerts listened to the music, so my store became the place to play."

Izzy began writing a column in *Sing Out!*, the folk music magazine, and, later created a newsletter called *The Folklore Center Continuing Folk Festival*. This featured, in equal measure, information on upcoming Folklore Center concerts and Izzy's salty opinions on all kinds of subjects. In 1961, Izzy, John Cohen and Ralph Rinzler created a little organization called Friends of Old-Time Music (FOTM). Under the auspices of FOTM, great old-time country musicians, including performers who had recorded "hillbilly" records in the 20s and 30s and who had subsequently been forgotten, were brought to New York to perform to adoring audiences.

Izzy was utterly devoted to folk music and folk singers, and didn't have a business brain in his head. One folk singer reported that, when he walked into Izzy's store as a stranger, Izzy said, "Would you mind the store for awhile? I have to go to the bank."

Izzy was disorganized, and was careless about collecting and remitting sales tax. By the early 1970s, the authorities were hounding him. In 1973, he left New York for Stockholm. He now runs a Folklore Center there, and returns to the U.S. for special folk events. Every folk singer of his generation knows and idolizes him. I owe him a special debt. I bought my first dulcimer at the Folklore Center soon after it opened.

Izzy Young in the Folklore Center, c. 1959. Photo by Photo-Sound Associates. Used with permission.

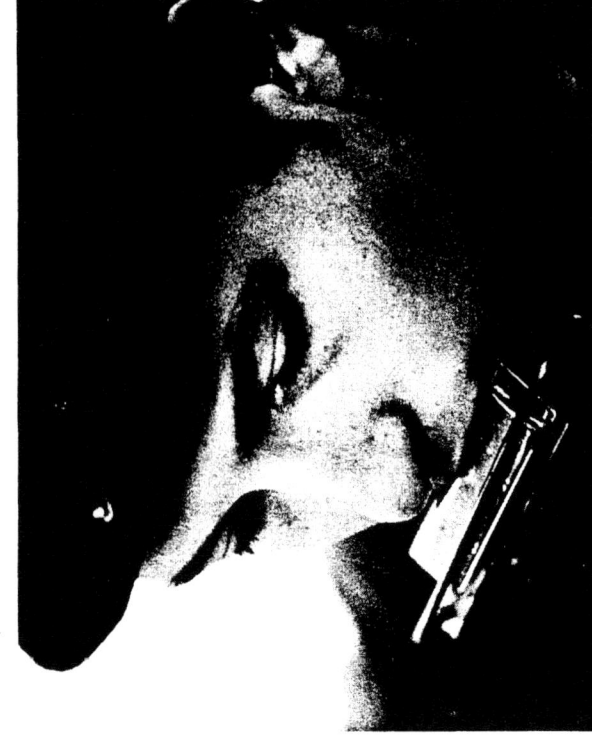

THE FOLKLORE CENTER

Presents

BOB DYLAN

IN HIS FIRST NEW YORK CONCERT

SAT. NOV. 4, 1961 **8:40pm**

CARNEGIE CHAPTER HALL
154 WEST 57th STREET • NEW YORK CITY

All seats $2.00

Tickets available at: The Folklore Center
                                     110 MacDougal Street
                                     New York City 12, New York

GR 7 - 5987   or at door

Newsletter

The Folklore Center is still open seven days a week from 12 noon. Mondays we close at seven, other days from 11pm to 2 am....Jimmy Gavin plays the role of Judasin a new passion play written by a Spaniard. "Automobile Graveyard" opns in two weeks....Martha Schlamme is signed exclusively with Verve Records....The Travelers Three signed exclusively with Elektra Records....Odetta goes to Europe to do TV in Holland, Sweden, France, etc. and will return in January....We have very few copies left of "The Bosses' Song Book @ $.75. Thye have been sold on the black market for as much as $2.00..... The Society for the Advancement of College Arts and Sciences present Oscar Brand in a "Folk song report" presenting Winnie Winston, Jane Reger, Larry Sandberg, Jon Lipsky, Kay Billig, Artie Traum and Mike LEssac, on Friday Nov. 24: 8:30pm. at Hunter College Assembly Hall. Tickets 1.50, 1.75, 2.00 and 2.50 available at the Folklore Center, Gr7-5987.....W recommend Pete Seeger's new "HOW TO PLAY THE 5-STRING BANJO. It is a tremendous bargain at $2.00.... Write for our new paper back catalogue listing over 150 new paperbackbooks of folkmusic, folklore, etc. It will be ready bedore Thanskgiving.... W"'ve gotten some more copies of the "Leadbelly" 70 songs, with words, music. $2.00....Jack Ballard works full time, seven days a week at the store now. Please do not ask him to sing every time you come into the store....Alice/ Conklin, Theo Bikel's Secretary, was seen at Feenjon's recently enjoying herself to the guitar work of Steve Knight....It's easy to get on our mailing list...You must get Alan Lomax' new LFs of English Folk Music called Songs of seduction and Songs of Courtship. They were recorded in England with Peter Kennedy and display a marvelous variety and strength. On the Caedmon label. We don't play records inthe store but we will return your money if you2don't think they are great. List 6.00, our price 4.95 by mail,phone or in person....Ray Boguslav designed the cover for hisnew album on Monitor Records....Margrit Hagnauer is Herald at Arms for the Folklore Center and her new Crest will be unfurled at Christmas at a special ceremony.

The issue of the Folklore Center Newsletter *announcing Bob Dylan's first New York Concert, November 4, 1961. The information about Bob that appears in the flyer was supplied by Bob to Izzy Young. As far as anyone knows, some of it isn't true! Courtesy Israel Young.*

Bob Dylan

Bob Dylan was born in Duluth, Minnesota in 1941. He was raised in Gallup, N.M., and before he came to New York earlier this year, he lived in Iowa, South Dakota, North Dakota and Kansas. He started playing Carnivals at the age of fourteen, accompanying himself on guitar and piano. He picked up the harmonica about two years ago.

The University of Minnesota gave him a scholarship. He went there for some five months, attended some dozen lectures and left. He learned many blues songs from a Chicago street singer named Arvella Gray. He also met a singer, Mance Lipscomb, from the Brazos River country of Texas, through a grandson that sang rock and roll. He listened a lot to Lipscomb. He heard Woody Guthrie's album of DUST BOWL BALLADS in South Dakota. In fact, Bob Dylan has sung old jazz songs, sentimental cowboy songs, top forty Hit Parade stuff. He was always interested in singers and didn't know the term "folk music" until he came to New York.

"people have to name it something so they call it folkmusic—now very few people singing that way. Being taken over by people who don't sing that way. It's all right but don't call it folk music. Stuff I do is nearer to folkmusic. Now singing old blues and Texas songs. I don't want to make a lot of money, want to get along....I want to reach more people and have the chance to sing the kind of music I sing.....people have to be ready and have seen me once already. People often say first time that this isn't folkmusic. My songs aren't easy to listen to. My favorite singers are Dave Van Ronk, Jim Queskin and Rick Von Schmidt, Jack Elliott, Peter Stampfel, I can offer songs that tell something of this America, no foreign songs - the songs of this land that aren't offered over TV and radio and very few records."

"Groups are easy to be in. I've always learned the hard way. I will now, too. I dress the way I do becase I wantto dress this way and not because it is cheaper or easier.

"I started writing my own songs about four or five years ago. First song was to Brigit Bardot, for piano. Thought if I wrote the song I'd sing it to her one day. Never met her. I've written hillbilly songs that Cal Perkins from Nashville, Tenn. sings. I write Talking Blues on Topical things. "California Brown Eyed Baby" has caught on. Noel Stookey gave me the idea for the "Bear Mountain Song" I wrote it overnight but I wasn't there. Never sing it the same way twice because I never wrote it down.

* * * * * * * *

"No one is really influencng me now- but actually everything does. Can't think of anyone in particular now."

* * * * * * * *

THE   FOLKLORE   CENTER

ON THE OCCASION

of a new LP

by

M O L L Y   S C O T T

announces

an

A U T O G R A P H   P A R T Y

Sat. afternoon, Nov. 11, 1961 at the Folklore Center, 110 MacDougal St., from 3 to 5 pm.

Cider, apples and cheese will be offered at the stated time. Molly's new record, on the Prestige label, will be authorgraphed at the same time. All welcome

Sandal Shop Owner
Allan Block standing in front of his Sandal Shop with his daughter, Mony, in the 1960s. The Sandal Shop was a gathering place for those with a special interest in old-time Appalachian music. Photographer unknown.

Indian Neck Folk Festival
Allan getting off a tune with guitarist Artie Rose at the Indian Neck Folk Festival, 1959. Photo by Photo-Sound Associates. Used with permission.

Frank Glenn Dulcimer
Ralph playing his Frank Glenn dulcimer in the Sandal Shop, mid-1960s. He is sitting on a high wooden work counter, just where Bob Dylan sat a few years before! Photo by Bill Knight. Used with permission.

ALLAN BLOCK'S SANDAL SHOP

Allan Block, a native of Wisconsin, studied classical violin as a boy and teenager, arrived in New York about 1950, and dropped by the offices of People's Songs, which was an early postwar crossroads of folk music and political activism. Pete Seeger was there. "Do you have a place to stay?" Pete asked. "If not, you can stay at my place on MacDougal Street." Allan said a grateful yes, and slept on Pete's floor;

Allan learned that a leather shop at 171 West 4th Street was for sale. He bought the business for $500, and set himself up as a leather worker. Later, he expanded to the shop next door, which had domiciled a shoe repair business. The rent for the combined premises was $125. Allan quickly received orders for sandals, and sandal making became his main business.

In the late 1950s, Allan's skill with the violin reached the ears of John Cohen who, with Mike Seeger and Tom Paley, had formed a group called The New Lost City Ramblers. This group was embarked on a quest that differed from that of both the Washington Square singers and the coffeehouse performers. John, Mike and Tom spent countless hours listening to old 78rpm commercial "hillbilly" recordings of the 1920s and 1930s that were in the possession of several New York-area collectors. Some of the recordings were extremely rare, existing in only one or a few known copies. The three friends learned the songs, formed the Ramblers, sang and recorded the music in the styles and techniques of the old performers and groups, and, in 1964, published a book, *The New Lost City Ramblers Song Book*.

When the group was forming, John loaned Allan a tape of the Ramblers' music. Allan was soon fiddling, playing the banjo, and singing the material in his shop. Others of us dropped in, and loved the music as much as he did. Saturday afternoon became folk music time at the shop. There was no singer-songwriter music and scarcely any bluegrass. It was old-time mountain music, played in a style that approximated the original.

Bob Dylan dropped by several times during his early days in New York. He sat on the high work counter, smiling, saying very little, and soaking everything up like a sponge. One time, when Allan met him on the street, Bob was carrying his guitar.

"Why don't you spend a little time with that guitar, and really learn to play it?" Allan asked.

"I don't think I want to do music," Bob replied. "I think I want to write poetry!"

Allan might have been smart to ask him for a few specimens. In a rock and pop auction at Christie's on November 21, 2005, poems handwritten by Dylan in 1960 sold for $78,000!

Summer Weekend in Washington Square
A big crowd in Washington Square on a Summer Weekend. This fuzzy photo is from the contact sheet supplied to the author by the late Lee Hoffman. See the caption to the photo on page 8. Photo by Photo-Sound Associates. Used with permission.

Washington Square Fountain
Fun in the Washington Square fountain. The identity of the happy wetniks is not known. Photo by Andrew Alpern. Used with permission.

1959 Afternoon Jam
Dave Van Ronk, Bob Yellin and Roy Berkeley jamming in the Folklore Center, probably on a weekend afternoon, c. 1959. Maybe Bob isn't enjoying himself. He seems to be thinking, "Who let these tone-deaf birds in?" Photo by Photo-Sound Associates. Used with permission.

HAPPY SUMMER DAYS

I was an article writer in Greenwich Village in the 1960s, and wrote a few books.

On a typical Saturday morning in summer, I would wake up to the sounds of the street coming in through the open living room windows. I virtually never cooked. Instead, I went downstairs, crossed Jones Street, and entered Joe's Restaurant on the corner of Jones and West 4th Streets. Two eggs, potatoes, toast and coffee cost fifty cents, with ten cents more for a tip for Gloria, the waitress. After breakfast, I would go back up, sit myself down at my 1929 Royal typewriter, which had cut-glass panels on its sides, and work through the morning.

In the afternoon, I would take my dulcimer and cross the street, where Allan Block's glorious fiddle playing could already be heard emanating from the open doors of the Sandal Shop. In addition to Allan, players and singers would typically include Andy May and Allan's teenage daughter Rory on guitar, Kenny Kosek and Richard Blaustein on fiddle, John Burke on fiddle and old-time banjo, and Eric Nagler on banjo (See page 95). I played harmonica and dulcimer.

A big crowd would gather outside to listen. The sidewalk was narrow, and the crowd would block it completely and spill over into the street. As I approached, I would hold my dulcimer partially aloft. It was a safe bet that a majority of the listeners had never seen one. The crowd parted respectfully, and I entered the shop.

Through the afternoon, we played and sang. Players drifted in and out, while Allan alternately played, outlined customers' feet on pieces of cardboard on which they stood, ran his buffing wheel, and hammered rivets into sandals. In the evening, the playing and singing often continued in my apartment. Listeners included Freya Samuels, a gentle and beautiful pianist, who didn't sing or play our raucous stuff but loved the folk world. We were well supplied with cans of Tudor beer, the house brand of the A&P on Bleeker Street. It was incredibly cheap. "Ann Page" was the house brand for many A&P products, and we called our refreshment Ann Page beer.

In the afternoon on Sunday, I would cover the typewriter, and put key of D, key of G, and key of A harmonicas in my pocket. The singers and players would be out in force in Washington Square, with clusters of listeners gathered around each impromptu group.

I elbowed my way through three-deep starry-eyed young ladies, some of them just off the A train from the Bronx, fished out a harmonica, and off we went. For an hour or so we played, while the crowds increased. Then several of us might wander down MacDougal Street. Later, I sometimes went over to the Peacock Coffee House on Greenwich Avenue. I wrote part of my first book sitting on an ice cream chair at a little, heavy, dark oak pedestal table with a six-sided top, in a window alcove beside the door, that looked out over the summer evening Village scene. A piece of the Peacock's Viennese Rum Delight and a cup of espresso could keep me scribbling for a couple of hours! Virginia, the Peacock's longtime waitress, made the Rum Delight at home and brought it in each day. It cost 50 cents, but I had to have it!

March 29, 1950: Jean Ritchie's First Public Concert
Jean exiting the Greenwich Mews Playhouse in the Village, after her first public concert in New York City, March 29, 1950, sponsored by the Country Dance Society. The white flowers were from Alan Lomax and the roses from George Pickow, her husband-soon-to-be. Photo by George Pickow. Used with permission.

Singing Party
A singing party at 88 7th Avenue South, in the Village, George and Jean's first apartment. Jean is in the rear center, standing and leaning on the chair. To her right (the viewer's left) is Paddy Clancy, and seated directly in front of her is Tom Clancy, both of the singing Clancy Brothers. Robin Roberts, Alan Lomax's companion, is playing the guitar and singing. Oscar Brand is seated in the "director's chair," lower right. On Jean's left is the "portable" Magnacorder, with which George and Jean made their 1952-53 collection of folklore in England, Scotland and Ireland during Jean's Fulbright year. Photo taken by George Pickow in 1954. Used with permission.

Gerde's Folk City Concert
Jean playing at Gerde's Folk City, in a concert given to welcome the opening of the Folklore Center, April 1957. The young listener on the left is transported. Photo by George Pickow. Used with permission

THE DULCIMER IN GREENWICH VILLAGE

Jean Ritchie, Princess of the Dulcimer

Jean Ritchie's name is forever linked with the Appalachian dulcimer. Virtually single-handed, she introduced it into the Folk Revival, and has remained its most famous player for more than half a century. In the early 1950s, Jean and her husband, George Pickow, lived in Greenwich Village, at 88 Seventh Avenue South, a block south of Sheridan Square. They dropped by frequently on Sunday afternoons to enjoy and participate in the singing in Washington Square. In 1956, they moved to Long Island to raise their family.

The youngest of 14 children of a mountain family with deep roots in the early history of the Cumberlands, Jean was born and raised in the tiny town of Viper, Kentucky. Her father, Balis, owned and played a dulcimer made by the legendary Kentucky dulcimer maker, James Edward "Uncle Ed" Thomas.

Jean graduated *summa cum laude* from the University of Kentucky in 1946, majoring in social work. After graduation, she went to New York to take a job at the Henry Street Settlement, bringing with her a dulcimer made by old-time Kentucky dulcimer maker Jethro Amburgey, who made dulcimers in the Thomas pattern. Virtually no one that she met or knew had ever seen a dulcimer or heard one played. The instrument fascinated and charmed everyone, and it quickly ran away with her life. She received invitations to perform and, in 1950, a small new record company, Elektra, invited her to be its first folk artist. In 1952-53, she received a Fulbright grant to travel to England and Scotland, to research the origins and sources of her family's music. Since then she has received myriad honors and awards, including the National Endowment for the Arts National Heritage Fellowship, the country's highest honor in the traditional arts.

In the 1950s, Jean, George and George's uncle, Morris Pickow, began to make and sell "Jean Ritchie dulcimers." The instruments were made by Morris, finished by George, and tuned by Jean. They made 357 numbered instruments, signed by Jean, which played a prominent role in popularizing the dulcimer in the Folk Revival. The Folklore Center often had one or two for sale. You can see Jean Ritchie dulcimer #228, purchased at the Folklore Center, on the next page.

Sometime in the latter part of the 1950s, I had my first opportunity to see and hear Jean perform. She and Washington Square banjo player Roger Sprung gave a concert at the Circle in the Square theatre on Sheridan Square. With Roger providing quiet, tasteful accompaniment on some pieces, Jean played simple Cumberland Mountain tunes such as "Shady Grove" and "Jubilee." For me, the impact was permanent.

Jethro Amburgey Dulcimer
Left: Jethro Amburgey dulcimer #495, dated 7/10/62, ordered by mail from Jethro Amburgey, Hindman, Kentucky, by Greenwich Village folkie Jane Greenman. The instrument is now owned by a collector, who treasures it.

Frank Glenn Dulcimer
Center: Dulcimer made by Frank Glenn, Beech Mountain, North Carolina, 1950s, purchased by Ralph at the Folklore Center, late 1950s.

Jean Ritchie Dulcimer
Right: Jean Ritchie dulcimer #228, signed by Jean and dated 1968. Made by Jean, her husband, George and George's uncle, Morris Pickow. Purchased by Ralph at the Folklore Center, 1968.

THE DULCIMER IN GREENWICH VILLAGE
Three Village Dulcimers

The instrument on the left in the photo on the facing page, made by Jethro Amburgey of Hindman, Kentucky, was ordered from Amburgey by young Village folkie Jane Greenman. I think he charged her $35 for it, shipped it in a handmade wooden case, and told her that she could return it if she didn't like it! According to my recollection, Jane brought it down to a MacDougal Street basket house called The Basement, played it, passed the basket, and did just fine.

The instrument in the middle was my first dulcimer. Sometime before 1960, Roger Abrahams, a young folkie who lived on Spring Street, returned from a field trip to North Carolina with a number of dulcimers and fretless banjos. He put several of them in the Folklore Center; I think that the price was $30 each. I bought the dulcimer shown here, and it was my working dulcimer in the Village for about ten years. In the 70s, I traveled to western North Carolina to learn who had made it. I found that the maker was Frank Glenn of Sugar Grove, North Carolina, a relative of the well-known dulcimer makers, Leonard and Clifford Glenn. Frank died in 1960, and his dulcimers are rare.

The dulcimer had many adventures in my ignorant hands. I had the historic old wire staple frets replaced with modern instrument frets, a decision that I later much regretted. I broke the beautiful pegs by trying to string it with guitar strings. Peter Carbone, the Village instrument maker and restorer, replaced them with viola pegs. In the 70s, Clifford Glenn made perfect duplicates of the beautiful originals for me. The instrument's sound is preserved on two cuts of an Elektra record entitled *Old Time Banjo Project*, EKL 276, issued in 1964, on which I play "Mississippi Sawyer" with Allan Block and "Paddy on the Turnpike" with Bill Vanaver. It isn't bad at all!

Throughout the 60s, I knew only two tunings, Ionian/DAA and Dorian/DAG. This confined me to the key of D. In the Sandal Shop, banjo and guitar players played many songs in G, and fiddlers generally played in D or A tunes. I waited for D tunes, and played harmonica on the others.

When I visited the Folklore Center, which was often, one or two Jean Ritchie dulcimers were frequently hanging there, for sale. "I don't need a dulcimer," I said to myself. "I have one!" But I looked at those beautiful instruments longingly. In 1968, I finally collapsed. I gave Izzy his $75, and brought home with me the instrument shown in the photo, on the right. It can be seen in the picture on page 6 that was taken in my 4 Jones Street apartment in 1969. It is an instrument of exceptional beauty, with tone to match. I played it on the album, *Ralph Lee Smith and Allan Block*, issued on 1972. Today, I still use it in concerts and historic presentations. People sometimes say, "That's an important instrument – you shouldn't be carrying it around!" I reply, simply. "I can't do without it!"

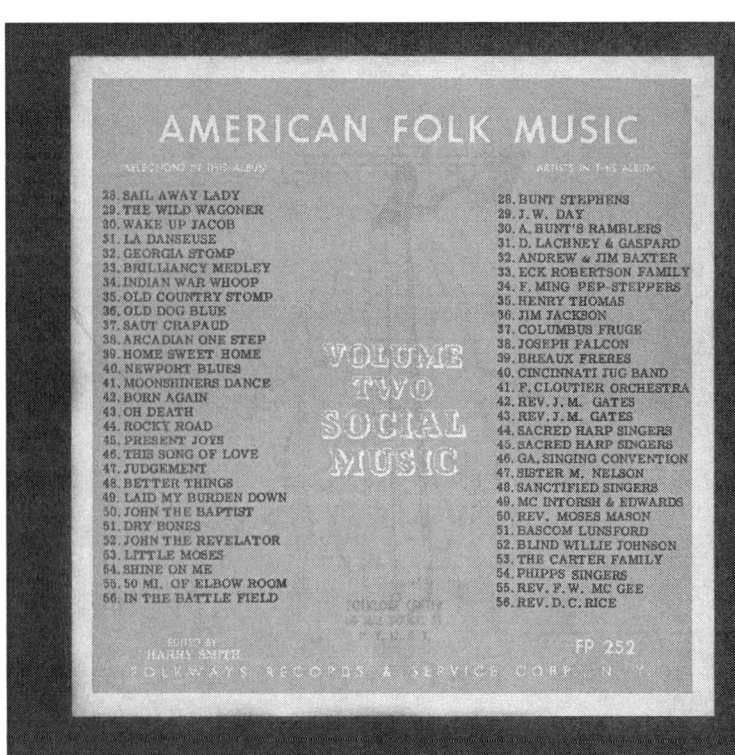

American Folk Music Vol. 2
Ralph's Village copy of Volume 2 of the Anthology of American Folk Music. *This set consisted of three boxes, each containing two LPs and a booklet. Ralph bought a set at the Folklore Center in the late 1950s. Used with permmission of Smithsonian Folkways.*

A County Album
An early County Records release. The County albums, put together through indefatigable searching for original 78rpm recordings, and accompanied by fascinating notes based on immense amounts of research, put Burl Ives and Joan Baez out of business forever in the Sandal Shop. Used with permission of County Records.

County Records Founder
Dave Freeman, founder of County Records. Photo taken by Carl Fleischhauer at the Carter Stanley Memorial Festival, McClure, Virginia, May 1972. Used with permission.

THE LITTLE RECORD COMPANIES

During my days in the Village, we were the beneficiaries of a revolution in the recording and re-release of authentic American folk music. Most of this activity was carried out by little record companies, especially in the earlier days of the Folk Revival. Several of these companies started in the Village. All of them poured authentic American folk music into the excited hands of the players in the Sandal Shop.

The grandfather of the small companies was Folkways Records, founded by Moses Asch in 1947. In 1952, Folkways issued a set of six LPs in three boxes with an accompanying 28-page booklet, the whole package entitled *Anthology of American Folk Music*. The *Anthology* was compiled by a wonderfully eccentric abstract film producer named Harry Smith, from his personal collection of old 78-rpm records from the 20s and 30s. The *Anthology* gave a tremendous boost to the Folk Revival. It provided me, and many others, with our first opportunity to hear to such traditional performers as Dock Boggs, Clarence Ashley, Uncle Dave Macon, and the Carter Family.

In 1950, Jac Holzman, a dropout from St. John's College in Annapolis, launched Elektra Records. Its original offices were at 361 Bleeker Street in the Village. Elektra's early releases included Jean Ritchie's first record. Elektra didn't stay little. Under Jac's skillful guidance, it followed the trend toward rock and cashed in. Jac moved to Hawaii. Back in the Village, a tale floated through the Folklore Center that he had bought an inter-island airline. If he didn't, he could have.

In the 1950s, young folk enthusiasts began to make trips to the Southern Appalachians, with recording equipment. This resulted in the issuance of albums by little companies, some of whose principals were the field collectors and/or performers themselves. Diane Hamilton, and Liam Clancy of the folk singing Clancy Brothers, founded one of these companies, Tradition, in 1956. Tradition's office was on the second floor of a building at 131 Christopher Street.

The advent of County Records in 1963-64, and of County Sales a year or two later, was the best news of all for lovers of authentic old-time music. Both companies were launched by Dave Freeman, whose dad ran an art gallery in the East 30s. Under the County label, Dave issued living country and old-timey artists, and reissued old-timey 78s of the 1920s and 1930s. County Sales was a mail order operation that sold both County records and releases by other companies, most of them hard to obtain. Dave stored records and shipped orders in a room in the back of the art gallery until the activity outgrew the space.

County Sales issued lists of records for sale, and a monthly *Newsletter*, listing, describing and offering books, pamphlets, and records issued by County and other companies, and providing news of the old-timey music scene. In the Sandal Shop, we shared the latest *Newsletter* and lists, and ordered a lot more than we could afford. We listened, enthralled, and we learned.

THE SANDAL SHOP MUSIC PRESERVED

In 1970, two young folk enthusiasts, Leslie Hansen and Isak Breslauer, started a little record company called Meadowlands Records. They asked Allan Block and me if they could record us, and we agreed. Some of the cuts on the album were recorded on portable equipment at the 1971 Indian Neck Folk Festival, and the rest were recorded at WNYU, the New York University student radio station.

The resulting record, *Allan Block and Ralph Lee Smith*, Meadowlands MS-1, is the only record ever made that flowed directly out of the music played in Allan Block's Sandal Shop in the 1960s. Six songs in this book – "Charley's Neat," "The Dying Ranger," "Finger Ring," "Georgia Railroad," "Roll on the Ground," and "Who's Going to Shoe Your Pretty Little Foot," come from this record.

LET'S PLAY AND SING AGAIN!

Sound like a dream? Well, it was! About 1970, Cynthia Gooding, a fine recording artist who specialized in international folk music, visited Izzy and had brunch with him at 321 Sixth Avenue, where the Folklore Center moved from MacDougal Street sometime in the 1960s. Izzy, a good cook, made breakfast for them. "Izzy," Cynthia said, as they ate together, "wouldn't it be wonderful if we could do it all over again?"

Friends, I'm sorry you couldn't be there, but singing and playing the songs is the next best thing. This book contains a selection of old-time songs we played and enjoyed in Allan Block's Sandal Shop in the late 50s and the 60s, with dulcimer tablature, a line of musical score, and guitar chords, all provided by Virginia folk singer Madeline MacNeil.

As you sing and play, think of Washington Square, and Izzy Young's Folklore Center, and Allan Block's Sandal Shop, and the MacDougal Street coffeehouses and basket houses, and the *Anthology*, and the County Sales *Newsletter*, and Ann Page beer, and Joe's, and those pretty young ladies from the A train!

Box Dulcimer
Ralph with a box dulcimer, at the Indian Neck Folk Festival, 1969. Photo by Photo-Sound Associates. Used with permission.

VILLAGE SCRAPBOOK

Outer panel of the Café Wha? Menu, 115 MacDougal Street, c. 1960

TAKE NOTICE

The Continuing Folklore Center Folk Festival

presents

THE KNUCKLEBUSTERS

vs

THE STAR SPANGLED STRING BAND

in an

E X T R A V A G A N Z A

of

fiddling, banjo picking, nice clean runs and sweet melodies,

followed by a fist fight between the principals:

Richard Blaustein

Ken Koseck

Andy May

Ralph Lee Smith

John Burke

| Monday, May 22, 1967, 8:30 p.m. |

ALL TICKETS $1.50, INCLUDING THOSE WITH THE BEST VANTAGE

the folklore center
321 Sixth Avenue
by Third Street
eight short blocks from St. Vincent's Hospital

sole proprietor - Israel G. Young

5th String banjo capos, large "A" tuning forks, autoharp wrenches, high grade rosin, and other weapons must be checked at the door before entrance.

Flyer for Folklore Center Concert, May 22, 1967. We never missed a chance for some nonsense! See the title page for a photo of the performance.

DAVE FREEMAN'S LP SALE LIST of COUNTRY MUSIC   1-OT

RCA VINTAGE 522 SONGS OF THE EARLY WEST Reissues of classic cowboy
    material from 1924-1931, with CARL T. SPRAGUE, JULES ALLEN, MAC
    McCLINTOCK, ECK ROBERTSON, GIRLS OF GOLDEN WEST, CARTWRIGHT
    BROTHERS, etc. 16 songs .... $ 3.75

RCA VINTAGE 507 SMOKY MOUNTAIN BALLADS reissues of the 1930s, with
    CARTER FAMILY, MAINERS, DIXON BROS., MONROE BROTHERS, ARTHUR
    SMITH, UNCLE DAVE MACON, etc. .... $ 3.75

```
========================================================================
= FP-828  THE LEGEND OF CLARK KESSINGER -- One of best fiddle LPs    ==
=    ever put out. Though 70 years old, Clark is without doubt       =
==   better today than even his early recordings of the 1920s.       =
=    18 great tunes accompanied by guitar & banjo. RED BIRD, SALT    =
=    RIVER, SALLY JOHNSON, TURKEY KNOB, SANDY RIVER, LEATHER         =
=    BREECHES, RICHMOND, CHINKY PIN, etc. This is the work of a      =
=    real artist.          ............................$ 3.50       =
========================================================================
```

CAMDEN 898 MAPLE ON THE HILL more reissues of old-time material
    including MAINERS, BRADLEY KINCAID, CARLISLE BROTHERS, RILEY
    PUCKETT, DELMORE BROTHERS, UNCLE DAVE MACON............$ 2.00

DECCA 4404 CARTER FAMILY FAVORITES 12 fine sides from the 1930s.
    $ 3.25
DECCA 4557 CARTER FAMILY FAVORITES--Volume 2   same $ 3.25

FA 2349 THE McGEE BROTHERS & ARTHUR SMITH Good selection of
    songs, 20 in all, featuring fine fiddling & great banjo and
    guitar playing by SAM McGEE. ....$ 3.75

RBF 51 UNCLE DAVE MACON reissues of early material ....$ 3.75

STARDAY 205 BLUE SKY BOYS a fine LP of material taken from radio
    transcriptions of the 1940s. ....$ 3.25

STARDAY 269 BLUE SKY BOYS-PRECIOUS MOMENTS 12 newly recorded sacred
    songs done in the old style. No gimmicks on this LP. $ 3.25

FP-32 THE 28th GALAX FIDDLERS CONVENTION (1963) 17 songs from
    the contest. Mixture of old-time and bluegrass........$ 3.50

PREST. 14030 38th UNION GROVE FIDDLERS CONVENTION 16 songs,
    leans more toward Bluegrass. Good record............$ 3.75

++++++++++++++++++++++

All RCA VICTOR VINTAGE LPs...................$ 3.75
 "   FOLKWAYS 12"   ....$ 3.75
 "   PRESTIGE 14000 series ....$ 3.75
 "   CAMDEN & HARMONY   ....$ 2.00

All orders to: DAVE FREEMAN
               311 East 37 St.
               New York 16, N.Y.

A typical issue of Dave Freeman's LP Sale List of Country Music, undated, mid-1960s.

CARNEGIE HALL/76th Season

Friday evening, September 22, 1967, at 8:30

SING OUT! Magazine

presents

HOOTENANNY

John Bassett

Tim Buckley

Len Chandler

Pete Seeger

The Star Spangled String Band

and

A Special Section Presented by

New Voices from Broadside Magazine

Elaine White

Janis Ian

Tom Parrott

Will McLean

Singing Their Own Songs

The Star Spangled String Band goes to Carnegie Hall, with others including Pete Seeger and Janis Ian. Ralph was not a member of the Band, but substituted for band member Alan Feldman, who couldn't make it. Other band members were Andy May, John Burke, Richard Blaustein and Kenny Kosek.

CARNEGIE HALL SET

    Set begins with all the group going onstage except Ralph. After the first part of Arkansas Traveler has been played, Ralph comes on with suitcase, takes out harmonica, joins the playing.

(1) <u>Arkansas Traveler</u>.   D   1:35

    John and Ralph sit down on chairs on stage, take very relaxed attitude, light up pipe and cigar. Andy tells joke (?), introduces the players, then introduces next song.

(2) <u>Cold Winter's Night</u>.   D   2:40

    John then introduces the following song as a "medieval ballad."

(3) <u>Love Letters in the Sand</u>.   D   1:55

    Andy now plugs John's book, pulls joke about John's banjo playing.

    Ken then introduces next song.

(4) <u>Soldier's joy</u>.   D   2:05

    Alan then introduces next song, dedicating it to LBJ.

(5) <u>Dying Ranger</u>.   G   2:50

    Andy now plugs Monday night concert.

    Ralph introduces final song, dedicating it to Frank Hoback if he is in the audience.

(6) <u>Eight More Miles to Louisville</u>.   A   3:15

Set list for the Carnegie Hall concert. It was typed on my 1929 Royal typewriter at 4 Jones St. More nonsense!

FUTURE CONCERTS:

BOB COOPER**
wed nov 18   8:30pm $2.00

HAPPY & ARTIE TRAUM
mon nov 23   8:30pm $2.00

THE PENNYWHISTLERS
mon dec 7   8:30pm $2.00

J.D. CROW Bluegrass Band
mon dec 14   8:30pm $2.00
in advance, $2.50 at the door.

** at Folklore Center, 321 6th Ave
one flight up, at 3rd st
                          All other
concerts at Wash Sq Church
135 W 4th St. Information 989 8811

Martin Guitars acquired the Vega Banjo Company in Boston during the summer, and most recently Martin Guitars and Darco Strings have merged, and that's nice for we only stock Martin Guitars and our own label strings are made by Darco. We always have lots of Martins on hand, at 25% discount!!! And why don't you try a set of our light, extra-light or medium bronze guitar strings for two dollars a set including postage if you can't get to the store itself. We guarantee them completely as we have for the last five years. We have strings for 12 string guitar, banjo, monel guitar strings, silk and steel, bronze and silk and more. Write in. And cheap as we charge they are even cheaper in quantity.

Send self-addressed envelope for reprint of Israel Young's article in East Village Other, Vol 1, No 1, Oct '65 on Bob Dylan o r pick up your copy in the store.

THE FOLKLORE CENTER CONTINUING FOLK FESTIVAL

JOE HICKERSON
mon oct 19   8:30pm $2.00

MICHAEL COONEY**
wed oct 21   8:30pm $2.00

JOHN FAHEY
mon oct 26   8:30pm $2.00

JERRY JEFF WALKER &
   Don Brooks, Harmonica
   Gary White, Guitar
   Bob Stevenson, Piano
   & Surprises!!!
mon nov 2   8:30pm $2.00

ALY BAIN &
MIKE WHELLANS
mon nov 9   8:30pm $2.00

A TRADITIONAL BALLAD EVE:
The Iron Mountain String Band, Ralph Lee Smith, Alan Block & Toni Gross
mon nov 16   8:30pm $2.00

** at Folklore Center, 321 Sixth Ave.
   All other concerts at the Washington Square Church, 135 W. 4th St. Information 989 8811.

OPEN 12-8 PM MON-SAT

FOLKLORE CENTER &
FRETTED INSTRUMENTS
321 SIXTH AVENUE · 989-8811

Outer panels of a typical issue of the Folklore Center/Continuing Folk Festival Newsletter. *In the listing of upcoming concerts, Allan and Ralph are listed for "A Traditional Ballad Eve" on November 18th. The Newsletter doesn't say what year, and Ralph doesn't remember!*

874 LANCASTER AVE. BRYN MAWR, PA. 19010 ▲ PHILA'S LARGEST FOLK CLUB ▲ PHONE (215) LA5-3375

PERFORMER'S AGREEMENT WITH THE
MAIN POINT

DATE *6/15/67*

I, *Bill Scarborough* AND THE MAIN POINT, 874 LANCASTER AVENUE, BRYN MAWR, PENNSYLVANIA MAKE THIS CONTRACT FOR THE PERSONAL SERVICES OF *Ralph Smith + the Strict Tempo Dance Band* ON THIS DATE, FOR THE PURPOSE OF EMPLOYMENT AT THE MAIN POINT *(min 5 musc.)* AT THE AFORE MENTIONED ADDRESS ON THE FOLLOWING DATES: *July 27, 28, 29, 30/67*

THE WAGE AGREED UPON IS THE FOLLOWING SUM: *$100.00*

OTHER ITEMS

* FORWARD ALONG WITH THE CONTRACT PICTURES AND PRESS RELEASE INFORMATION.
* IF FROM OUT OF TOWN, PLEASE CALL UPON ARRIVING IN TOWN ON THE FIRST DAY. LA 5-9596
* IF YOU ARE GOING TO BE LATE, CALL BEFORE 7PM - LA 5-9596
* ACCOMODATIONS WILL BE ARRANGED IF REQUESTED TWO WEEKS BEFORE DATE.

1. If due to illness, accident, death, or other causes legally known as ACTS OF GOD, the performer is forced to cancel a contract, neither the performer, the manager, nor any other representative shall be liable for any amount over that paid to the performer as deposit.
2. There shall be no penalty if the performer is prevented from his (her or their) performance due to unlawful strike.
3. The performer's signature on this contract is binding on receipt of signed copy of contract.
4. The performer is expected to be on the premises at least thirty (30) minutes before going on stage at showtime.

Showtimes *8 + 10 plus 11:30 Fri + Sat - 30 min sets*

xxx PLEASE RETURN ONE COPY OF THIS CONTRACT, SIGNED, TO THE MAIN POINT PRIOR TO YOUR ENGAGEMENT.

xxx PERFORMER'S SIGNATURE _____

SPONSOR _____ (FOLKLORE, INC. & THE MAIN POINT)
BY *M Scarborough* THE MAIN POINT

I can arrange accomodations at $13 for 5, or $15 for 6 per night and this includes breakfast. These arrangements can be made for any nu when you get here.

How not to get rich playing folk music! This contract for a performance at the Main Point Coffee House in Bryn Mawr, Pa., calls for a minimum of five musicians to perform for four nights, two shows on Wednesday and Thursday and three shows on Friday and Saturday, all for $100. And we paid our own expenses! But never mind, Arlo Guthrie was on the bill with us! He sang "Alice's Restaurant," the 25-minute song that made him famous.

WELL, FOR GOSH SAKES!
THEY'RE BACK IN WASHINGTON SQUARE!

On Christmas Day, 2003, in Brooklyn, New York, a disabled New York banjo player named Lou Giambattruzzi sat in his wheelchair and sent out email invitations to join a new listserv that he called New York Bluegrass and Old Timey (NYBGOT). The qualification for joining was, simply, having played bluegrass and/or old timey music in New York. Some 125 persons signed on, including many who, when they were young, had played in Washington Square on Sundays in the 50s and 60s.

The old-timers in NYBGOT quickly showed that they had lost none of their ability to cook stuff up. They organized a Reunion of the 50s and 60s Washington Square players, to take place in Washington Square on Sunday Afternoon, September 25, 2005. For those who came, it was unforgettable. Many had not seen each other for 40 to 50 years, and some had not even been in the Village for that long. It was quickly evident that they hadn't lost a bit of their playing skill. Just as in the old days, they gathered in impromptu groups and clusters, and the tunes flew. And, just as in the old days, park strollers and bystanders gathered, listened, and loved it. The Reunion of the Bluegrass and Old Time Washington Square players has now been set up to take place in the Park each year.

50s-60s Washington Square Reunion

This photo was taken in front of Washington Square Arch at the First Reunion of the 50s-60s Washington Square players in 2005. It shows once and for all that, when Ponce deLeon tramped through the Florida swamps looking for the Fountain of Youth, he was looking in the wrong place. He should have played folk music in Greenwich Village instead! Photo by Linda Camiel Butler. Used with permission.

THE SONGS

Washington Square Arch in early morning light. This fine photo was taken by Mike Nogami, about 6:00 a.m. on a summer morning. The night-time folk singers in the coffeehouses probably never saw it this early. Used with permission

Charley's Neat

Tune D A G
Strum (noter style)

Chorus:
Charley's neat and Charley's sweet,
And Charley he's a dandy.
Charley, he's the very same man
Who feeds the girls on candy.

Some folks marry for good looks,
Some folks marry for money,
But I'm goin' to marry a pretty little girl,
Kiss her and call her honey.

I don't want none of your weevily wheat,
Don't want none of your barley;
Take some flour and half an hour
To bake a cake for Charley.

Pappa's gone to New York town,
Mamma's gone to Dover,
Sister's wore her slippers out
From kicking Charley over.

Under the title "Charley, He's a Good Ol' Man," this song appears in the *New Lost City Ramblers Songbook*, with two of the three verses that appear here and two that do not. The verse about kicking Charley over does not appear in the Ramblers' version. It drifted into the Sandal Shop and made itself at home! "Charley's Neat" is an old play-party song, with links that go back to Bonnie Prince Charlie and the 1745 Jacobite Rebellion.

Finger Ring

Tune D A A
Strum

Chorus:
Finger ring, my darling
Finger ring, my dear,
I wish I had a finger ring
I'd go away from here.

Finger ring, my darling
Shines like any gold,
Wish't I had a finger ring
Since I was eight years old.

I wish I had some whiskey
I wish I had some rum;
I wish I had a bottle of corn
I'd sure give Nancy some.

Yonder there's a rabbit
Settin' in the sand;
If'n he don't get out of there,
I'll fry him in my pan.

I went across the mountain,
Crossed it in the spring;
And when I got to the other side
You could hear my banjo ring.

Allan Block and Ralph learned this simple, charming song from Virginia traditional singers Harry and Jeanie West, who arrived in New York in the 1950's, made several early folk recordings with Folkways, and were an important influence in the burgeoning revival of interest in old-time Appalachian music. Harry and Jeanie recorded "Finger Ring" on *Good Old Mountain Dew*, issued by Washington Records. It appears on *Allan Block and Ralph Lee Smith*, with Allan on banjo, Rob Fleder on guitar, and Ralph on harmonica. Some of the verses here are from Harry and Jeanie, and some just floated into the Shop.

Finger Ring

Tune D A D
Strum

Italic tablature numbers: Melody is on the middle string. Strum all of the strings, but emphasize the middle string.

Chorus:
Finger ring, my darling
Finger ring, my dear,
I wish I had a finger ring
I'd go away from here.

Finger ring, my darling
Shines like any gold,
Wish't I had a finger ring
Since I was eight years old.

I wish I had some whiskey
I wish I had some rum;
I wish I had a bottle of corn
I'd sure give Nancy some.

Yonder there's a rabbit
Settin' in the sand;
If'n he don't get out of there,
I'll fry him in my pan.

I went across the mountain,
Crossed it in the spring;
And when I got to the other side
You could hear my banjo ring.

Dance All Night With A Bottle In Your Hand

Tune D A A
Strum

Dance All Night With A Bottle In Your Hand

The tune of this song is on a record entitled *Music for Moonshiners, Played and Sung by the Laurel River Valley Boys*, field-recorded in North Carolina in 1957 by a young folkie, Kenneth Goldstein. (Kenny later got a Ph.D. and became an important academic folklorist.) It was released by Judson Records, a small New York label. All of the tunes on this record are instrumentals, and Ralph cannot say where he picked up the words which appear here. The first verse obviously belongs to the song, but the other two are floating verses. This is an easy-to-play, swingy little fiddle tune and may have been played at dances, perhaps with one verse sung.

> Dance all night with a bottle in your hand,
> Dance all night with a bottle in your hand,
> Dance all night with a bottle in your hand,
> Just before dawn give the fiddler a dram.
>
> Who's been here since I've been gone? (3 times)
> Pretty little girl with a red dress on.
>
> I used to have a dog named Bill (3 times)
> If he ain't gone I got him still.

Dance All Night With A Bottle In Your Hand

Tune D A D
Strum

Italic tablature numbers: Melody is on the middle string. Strum all of the strings, but emphasize the middle string.

Way Down Town

Tune D A A
Strum

47

Way Down Town

Allan Block's daughter, Rory, loved this song, and still does! She sang it often in the Sandal Shop. Rory was a folk music prodigy. She recorded on the Elektra release, *Old Time Banjo Project*, in 1964, when she was fourteen. She went on to become a nationally and internationally proclaimed blues artist, with an especially large following in Europe. In the late 1990s, when Rory and Ralph met again, they played "Way Down Town" to their heart's content!

Well, it's way down town just fooling around
Took me to the jail;
And it's oh, me, and it's oh, my,
No one to go my bail.

I wish I was down at my sweet Sally's house
Sittin' in an old arm chair;
One arm around my old guitar,
And the other one around my dear.

Well, it's one old shirt is all I got
A dollar is all I crave;
I brought nothing with me into this old world,
Take nothing to my grave.

Rory Block
Rory Block, Allan Block's daughter, with her son Thiele. Photo taken in the Village in the 1970's. Rory became an internationally famous blues singer and guitarist. Photo by Bill Knight. Used with permission.

Way Down Town

Tune D A D
Strum

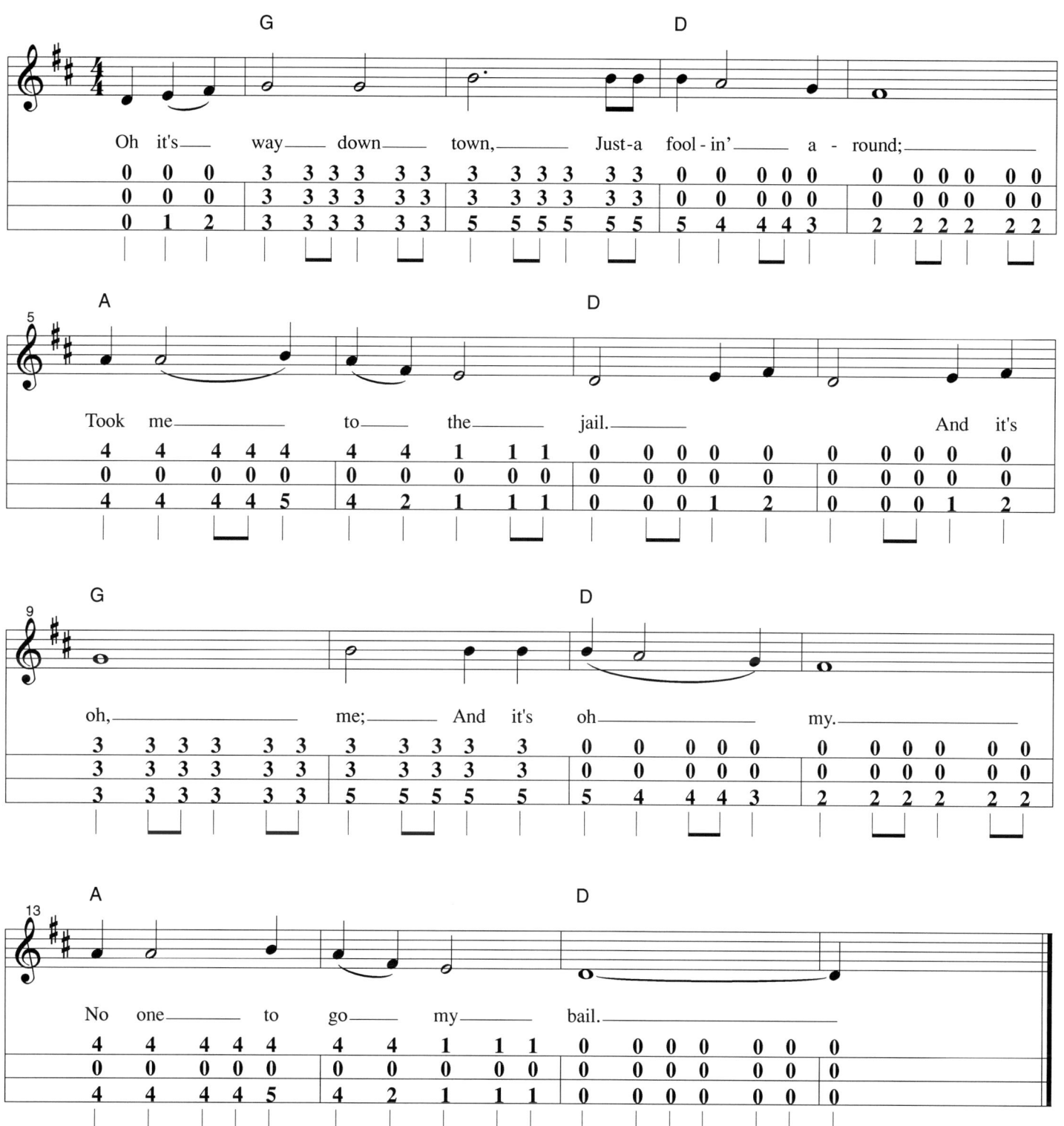

Additional verses on previous page.

Johnson Boys

Tune D A A
Strum

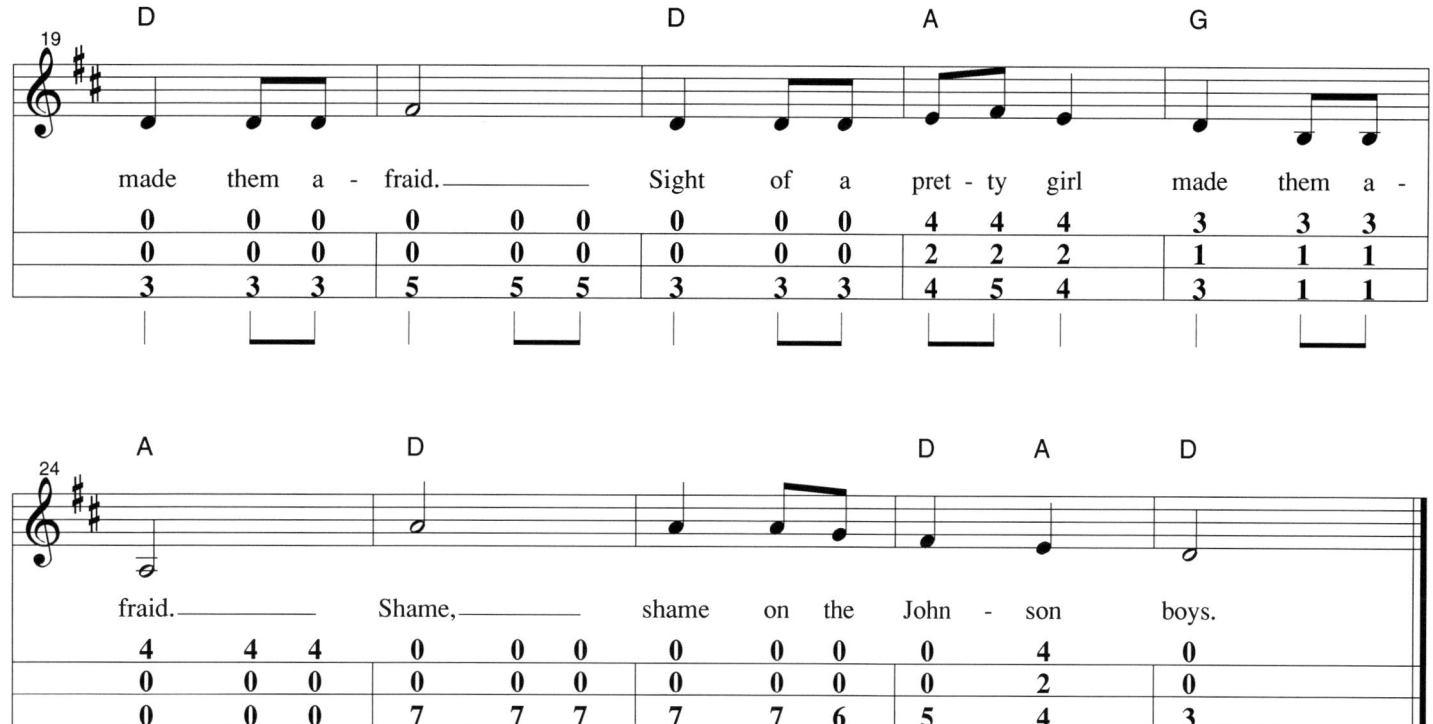

Johnson boys were raised in the ashes
Didn't know how to court a maid;
Turn their backs and hide their faces
Sight of a pretty girl makes 'em afraid.

Chorus:
(Last line of each verse, sung twice)
Shame, shame on the Johnson Boys.

Johnson boys, they think they're dandy
Johnson boys, they're long and thin;
Combed their hair and washed their faces
Look pretty good for the shape they're in.

Johnson boys went a-courtin'
Coon Creek girls so pretty and sweet;
They couldn't make no conversation,
They didn't know where to put their feet.

Johnson boys, they'll never get married
They'll stay single all their life;
They're too scared to pop the question
Ain't no woman goin' to be their wife.

Johnson boys, play your fiddle
Johnson boys, sing your song;
Johnson boys, hug 'em in the middle
Hug 'em in the middle and you can't go wrong.

    Poor Johnson Boys! The Sandal Shop folksingers never tired of recounting the boys' embarrassing woes, in Washington Square, the Sandal Shop, and at parties. The song was sung by a 1920s string band called The Hillbillies. There are many verses, but ones dealing with courting misadventures were favorites. Ralph learned the final verse of this version many years after his Village days, from the singing of North Carolina singer Frank Profitt, Jr. at the Dulcimer Playing Workshop at Appalachian State University in the early 1990s.

Johnson Boys

Tune D A D
Strum

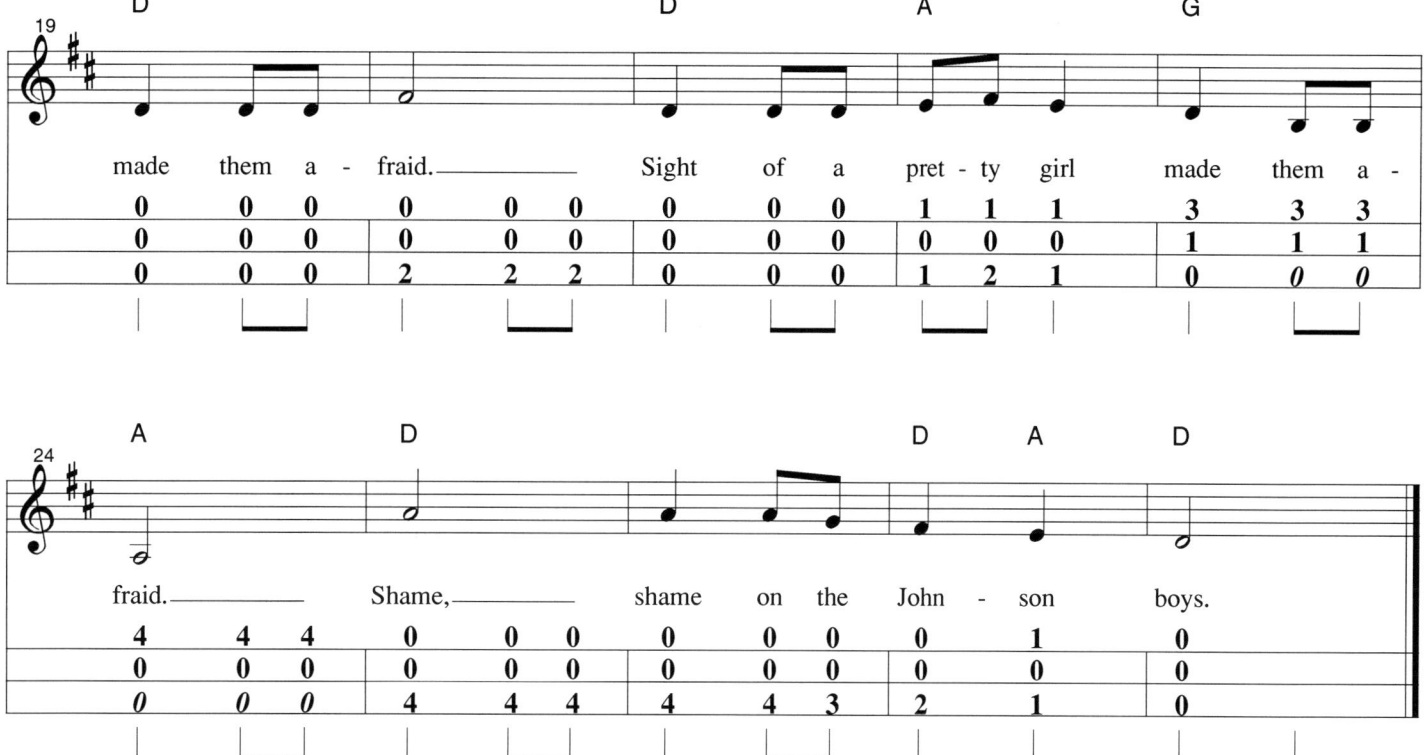

Italic tablature numbers: Melody is on the middle string. Strum all of the strings, but emphasize the middle string.

Johnson boys were raised in the ashes
Didn't know how to court a maid;
Turn their backs and hide their faces
Sight of a pretty girl makes 'em afraid.

Chorus:
(Last line of each verse, sung twice)
Shame, shame on the Johnson Boys.

Johnson boys, they think they're dandy
Johnson boys, they're long and thin;
Combed their hair and washed their faces
Look pretty good for the shape they're in.

Johnson boys went a-courtin'
Coon Creek girls so pretty and sweet;
They couldn't make no conversation,
They didn't know where to put their feet.

Johnson boys, they'll never get married
They'll stay single all their life;
They're too scared to pop the question
Ain't no woman goin' to be their wife.

Johnson boys, play your fiddle
Johnson boys, sing your song;
Johnson boys, hug 'em in the middle
Hug 'em in the middle and you can't go wrong.

The Dying Ranger

Tune D G D
Fingerpick

The Dying Ranger

This song was one of John Burke's favorites. On *Allan Block and Ralph Lee Smith*, Ralph sings it and plays it on harmonica, accompanied by Rob Fleder on guitar. Traditional sources of the song include Library of Congress record AAFSL28, *Cowboy Songs, Ballads, and Cattle Calls from Texas*, sung by John Prude at Fort Davis, Texas in 1942.

The sun was sinking in the west and it fell with lingering ray
Through the shadows of the forest where the wounded ranger lay.
'Neath the shade of a palmetto and sunset silvery sky,
Far from his home in Texas, we laid him down to die.

Draw closer to me, comrades, and listen while I say,
For I'm going to tell a story ere the spirit fades away.
Way back in northwest Texas, that good old Lone Star State,
There's one for whom my coming with a weary heart will wait.

A dear young girl, my sister, my only joy and pride,
I brought her up from childhood, I never left her side.
For her mother, she lies sleeping beneath the churchyard sod,
And her father, too, is resting in the bosom of our God.

I'm dying, comrades, dying, I must leave her all alone;
Who will be to her a brother, who will take her to his home?
Up spoke the noble rangers, they answered one and all;
We'll keep her as a brother 'till the last of us is called.

One last sweet smile of sorrow o'er the pain-wracked face had spread,
Then darkened into shadow and the ranger boy was dead.
Far from his darling sister we laid him down to rest,
With a saddle for a pillow, and a gun across his chest.

Little Moses

Tune D A A
Strum

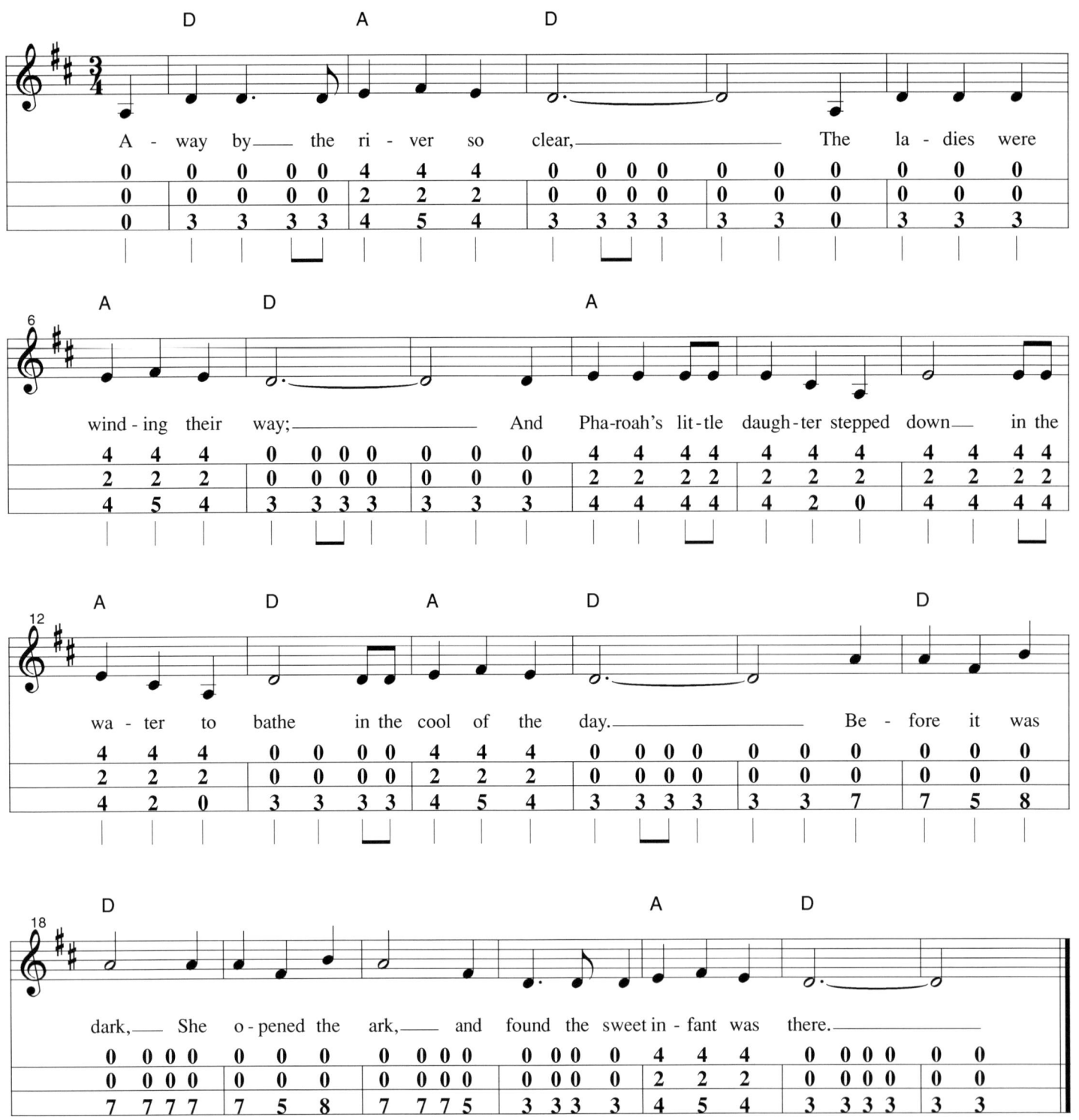

Little Moses

This is the second of the two Carter Family recordings that appear on the *Anthology of American Folk Music* (see headnote to "Single Girl"). It should be noted that the entire *Anthology* has recently been reissued by the Smithsonian Institution in CD format, with greatly augmented information and accompanying materials. According to Ralph's recollection, "Little Moses" was beautifully sung by Annie Bird, a 60s folk singer in the Village, whose voice bore a strong resemblance to that of Sara Carter. As with so many of Ralph's friends who passed through the folk singing world of the 60s Village, he does not know where Annie is. If you see this, Annie, contact him!

Away by the river so clear,
The ladies were winding their way;
And Pharoah's little daughter
Stepped down in the water
To bathe in the cool of the day.

Before it was dark, she opened the ark
And found the sweet infant was there.
Before it was dark, she opened the ark
And found the sweet infant was there.

And away by the waters so blue
The infant was lonely and sad;
She took him in pity
And thought him so pretty
And it made Little Moses so glad.

She called him her own, her beautiful son
And sent for a nurse that was near.
She called him her own, her beautiful son
And sent for a nurse that was near.

And away by the river so clear
They carried the beautiful child
To his own tender mother,
His sister and brother,
His mother so good did all that she could
To rear him and teach him with care.
His mother so good did all that she could
To rear him and teach him with care.

And away by the sea that was red
Little Moses, the servant of god,
While in him confided, the sea was divided
As upward he lifted his rod.

The Jews stepped across while Pharoah's host
Was drownded in the waters and lost.
The Jews stepped across while Pharoah's host
Was drownded in the waters and lost.

And away on the mountain so high
The last one that ever might see,
While in him victorious,
His hope was most glorious
He would soon o'er the Jordan be free.

When his labor did cease, he departed in peace
And rested in the heavens above.
When his labor did cease, he departed in peace
And rested in the heavens above.

Little Moses

Tune D A D
Strum

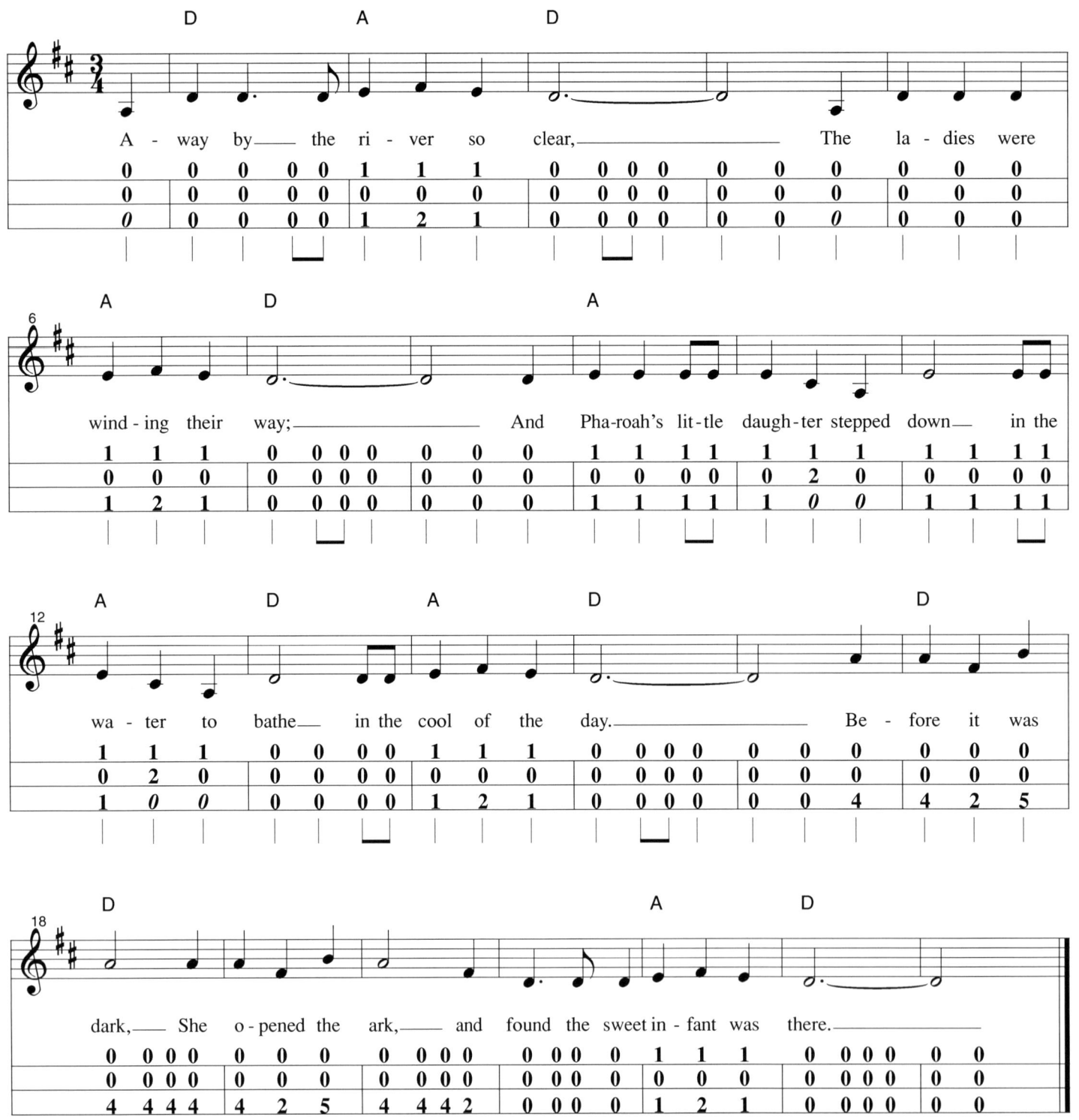

Italic tablature numbers: Melody is on the middle string. Strum all of the strings, but emphasize the middle string. Additional verses are on page 57.

Run Mountain

Tune D A A
Strum

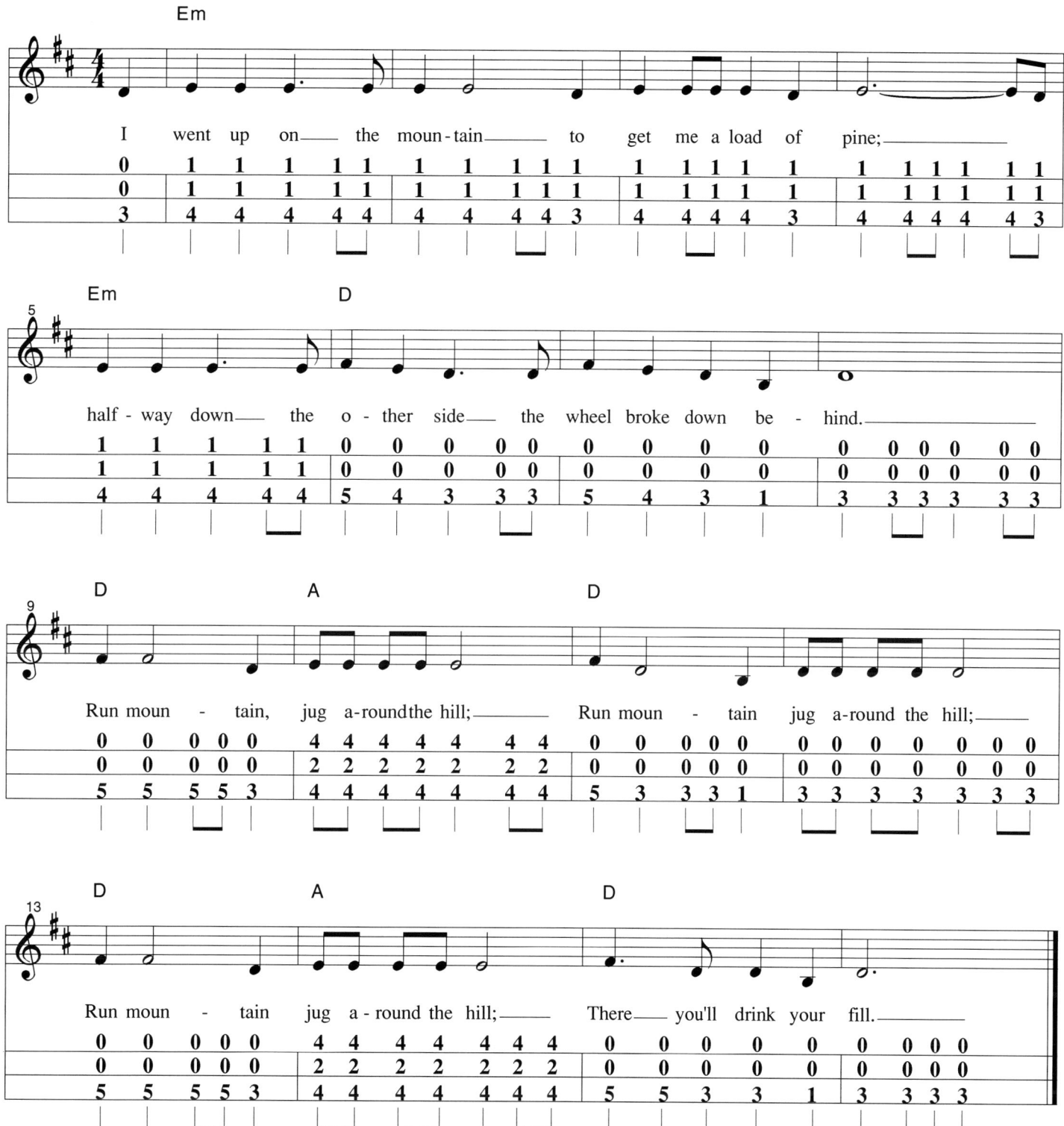

Run Mountain

    This is a most unusual tune. After the pickup measure the tune begins on the second note of the scale, which is E, harmonized with an E-minor chord. It shifts to the tonic chord in the sixth measure. This transition gives the tune a real "bite!" The song appears in the *New Lost City Ramblers Songbook*, with an attribution to J. E. Mainer's Mountaineers. The verses that Ralph remembers, which are given here, track the *Songbook's* verses only approximately, and the second verse is not in the *Songbook*.

I went up on the mountain
To get me a load of pine.
Halfway down the other side
The wheel broke down behind.

Chorus:
Run mountain, jug around the hill (3 times)
There you'll drink your fill.

Take my pack from off my back
My rifle off my shoulder;
Take me home from Mexico
I don't want to be a soldier.

Now I got no money
Got no place to stay;
I've got no place to lay my head
And the chickens a-crowin' for day.

When I was real hard at work
I worked both night and day;
Thinking of my old true love
She's many miles away.

Run Mountain

Tune D A D
Strum

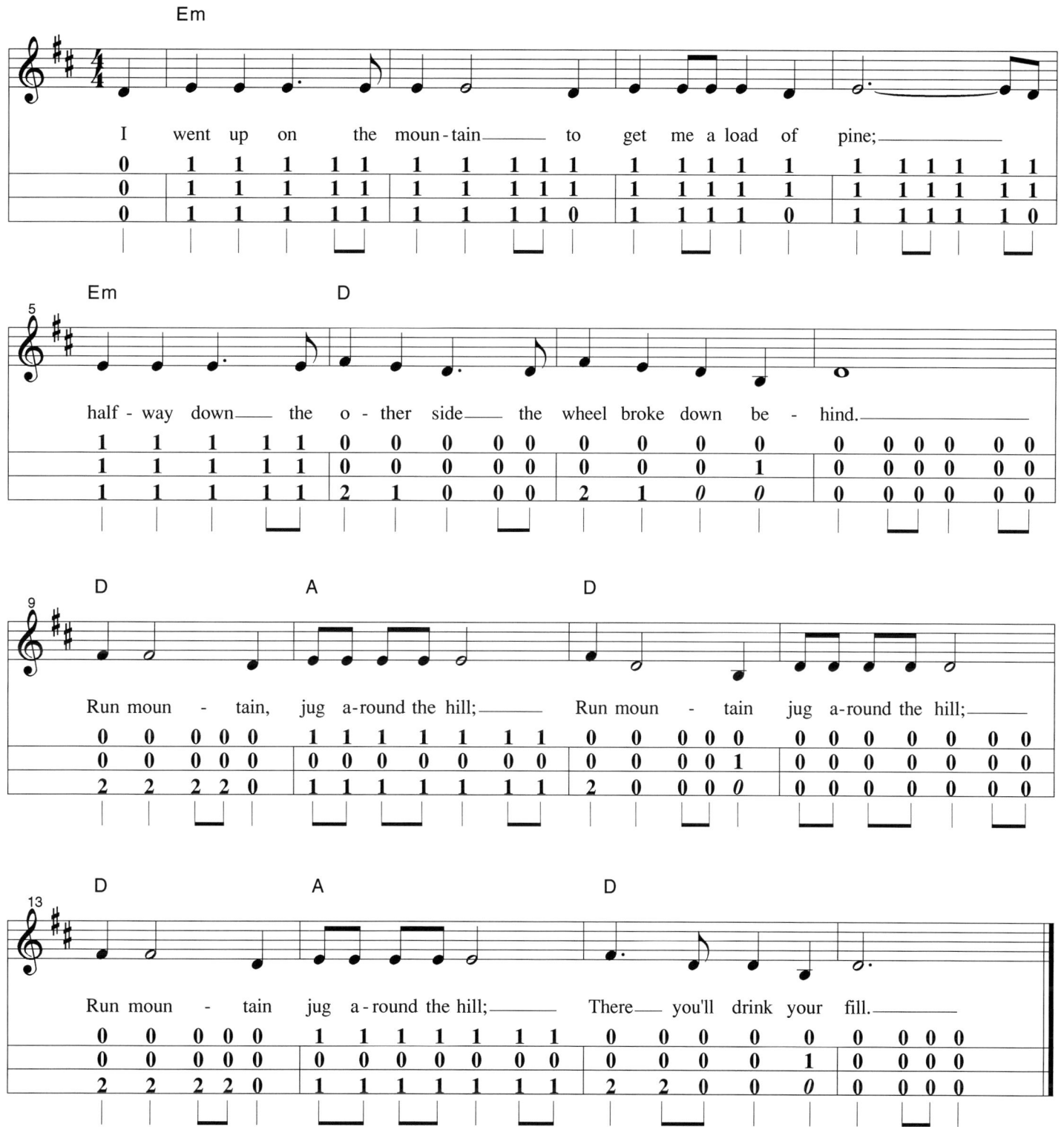

Italic tablature numbers: Melody is on the middle string. Strum all of the strings, but emphasize the middle string.

Roll In My Sweet Baby's Arms

Tune D A A
Strum

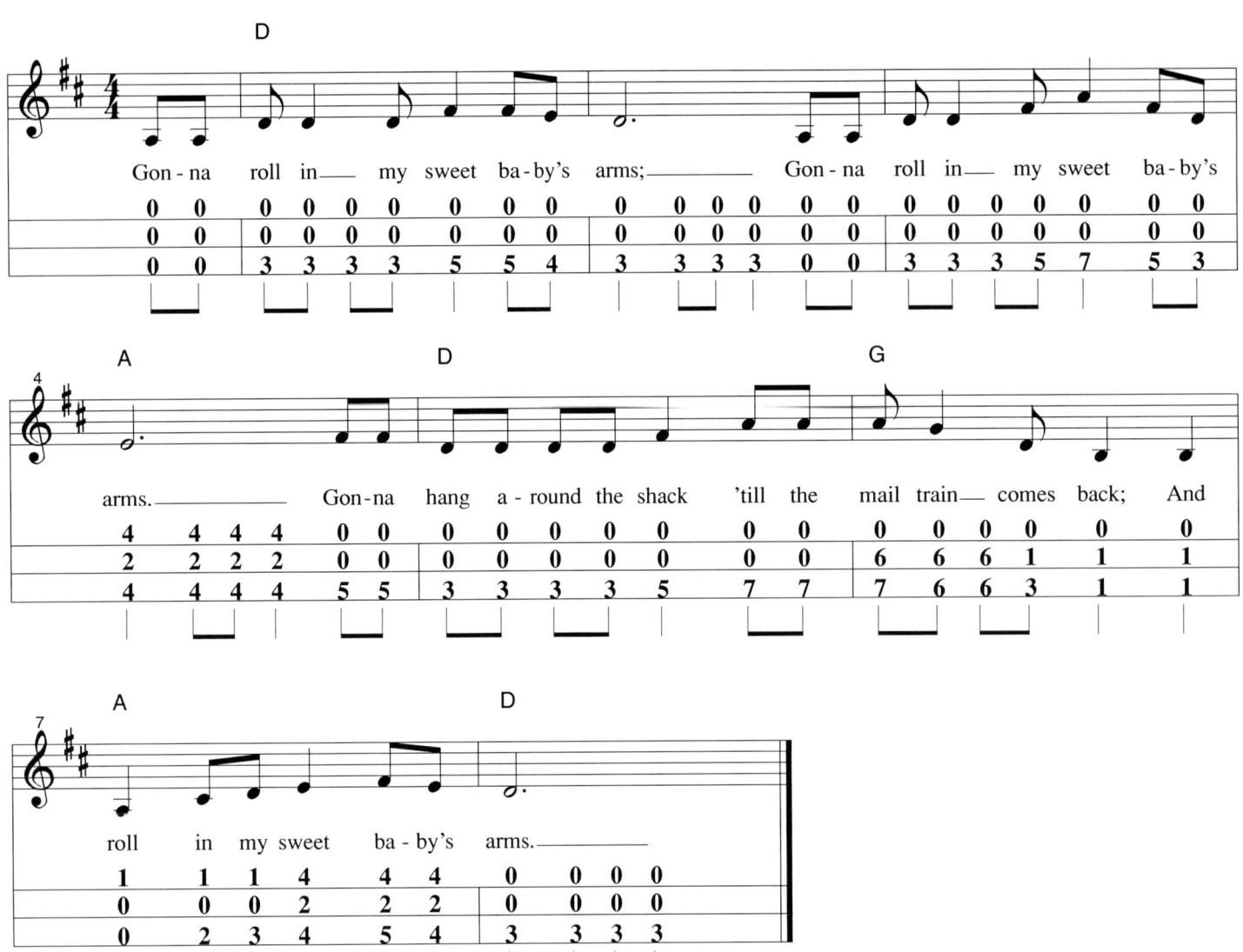

This tune is on the record *Music for Moonshiners*, field-recorded in North Carolina in 1956. (See the headnote for "Dance All Night With a Bottle in Your Hand.") All of the tunes on the record are instrumentals, but there was no problem about words for the song. They were known to virtually every Sunday afternoon player in Washington Square.

Roll In My Sweet Baby's Arms

Tune D A D
Strum

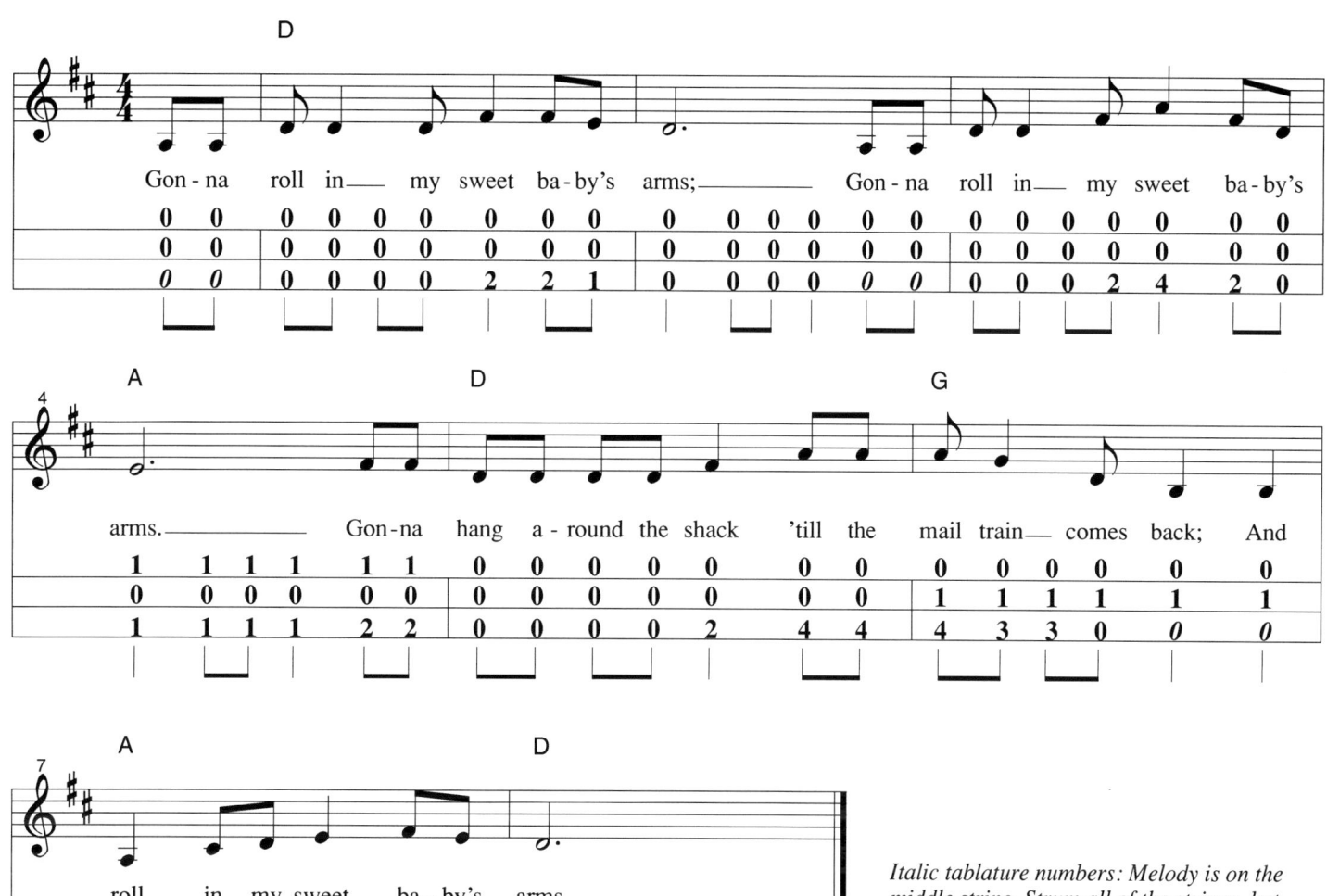

Italic tablature numbers: Melody is on the middle string. Strum all of the strings, but emphasize the middle string.

Chorus, at the beginning and after each verse:
Goin' to roll in my sweet baby's arms;
Goin' to roll in my sweet baby's arms.
Goin' to hang around the shack
'Till the mail train comes back,
And roll in my sweet baby's arms.

I ain't goin' to work on the railroad;
I ain't goin' to work on the farm.
Goin' to hang around the shack
'Till the mail train comes back,
And roll in my sweet baby's arms.

Well, where was you on Friday night;
When I was a-lying in jail?
You was goin' around town with another man,
And I didn't have no one to go my bail.

Single Girl, Married Girl

Tune D A A
Strum

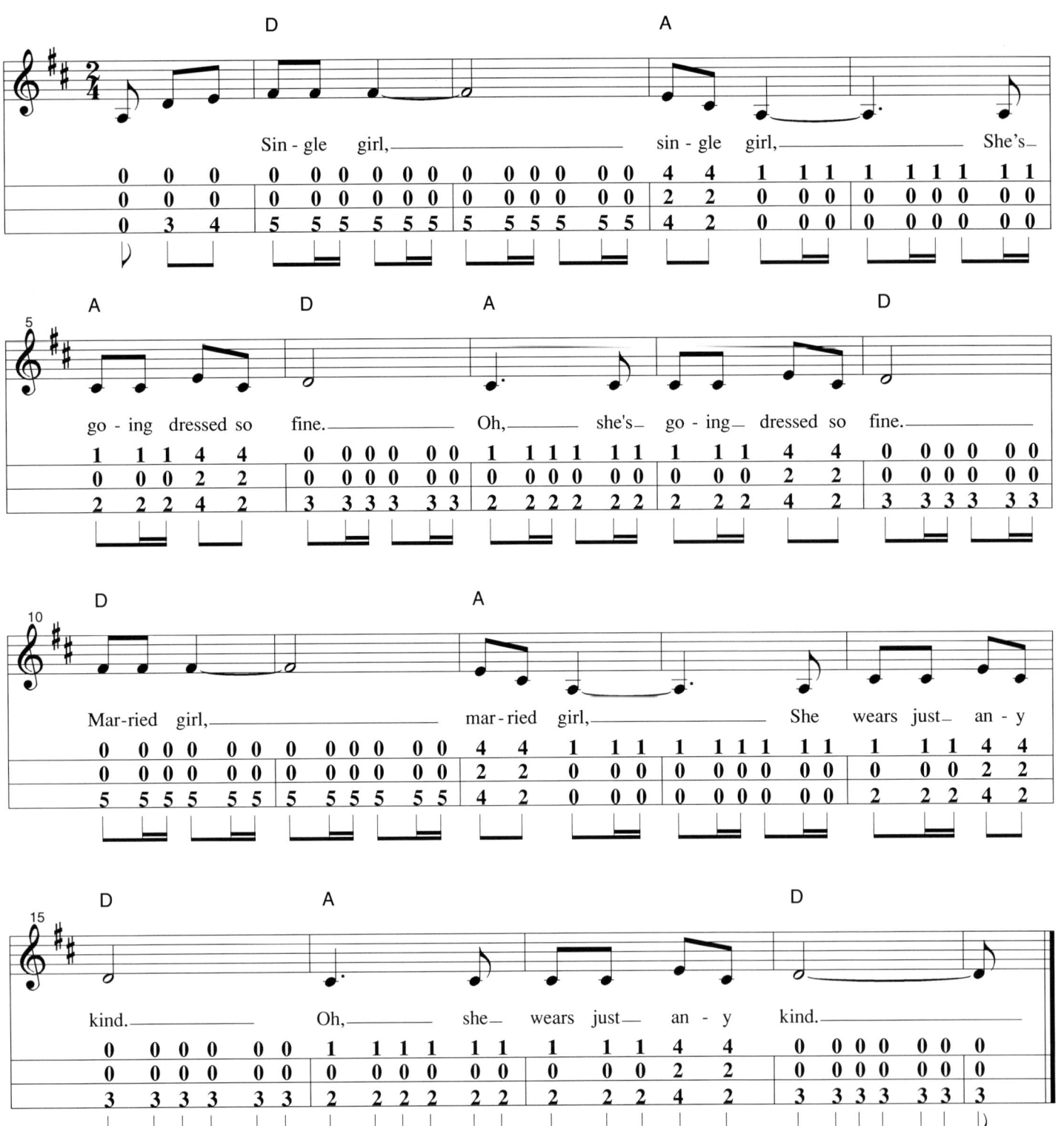

Single Girl

This is one of two Carter Family songs that appear on Harry Smith's seminal collection, *Anthology of American Folk Music*, released by Folkways on six LP's in three boxes in 1952 with a wonderful 28-page booklet. The other song is 'Little Moses,' which also appears in this book. Ralph still has the copies of Volumes 2 and 3 of the *Anthology* that he owned in the Village; Volume 1 is lost. Volume 2 is the original issue, with the box broken and in tatters. A rubber stamp on the front label reads, "Folklore Center, 110 Mac Dougal Street, N.Y. 12, N.Y." "Single Girl" and "Little Moses" were Ralph's introduction to the Carter Family. He sat spellbound in his apartment at 21 Jones Street and played the two cuts over and over!

Single girl, single girl
She's going dressed so fine,
Oh, she's going dressed so fine.
Married Girl, married girl
She wear just any kind,
Oh, she wears just any kind

Single girl, single girl
She goes to the store and buys,
Oh, she goes to the store and buys.
Married girl, married girl
She rocks the cradle and cries,
Oh, she rocks the cradle and cries.

Single girl, single girl
She's going where she please,
Oh, she's going where she please.
Married girl, married girl
Baby on her knees,
Oh, baby on her knees

Single Girl, Married Girl

Tune D A D
Strum

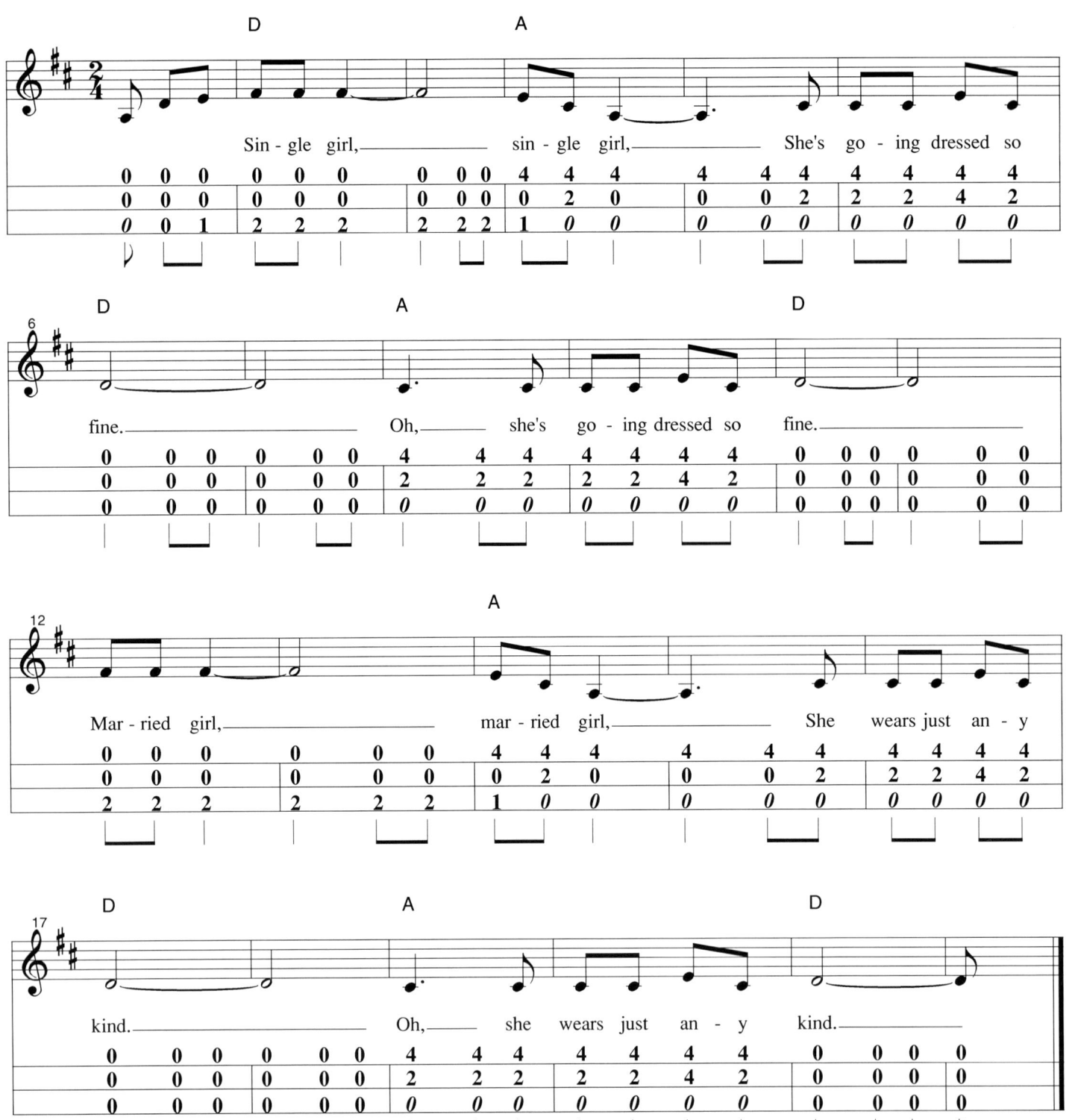

Italic tablature numbers: Melody is on the middle string. Strum all of the strings, but emphasize the middle string.

Chickens Are a-Crowin'

Tune D A G
Finger/Flat Pick

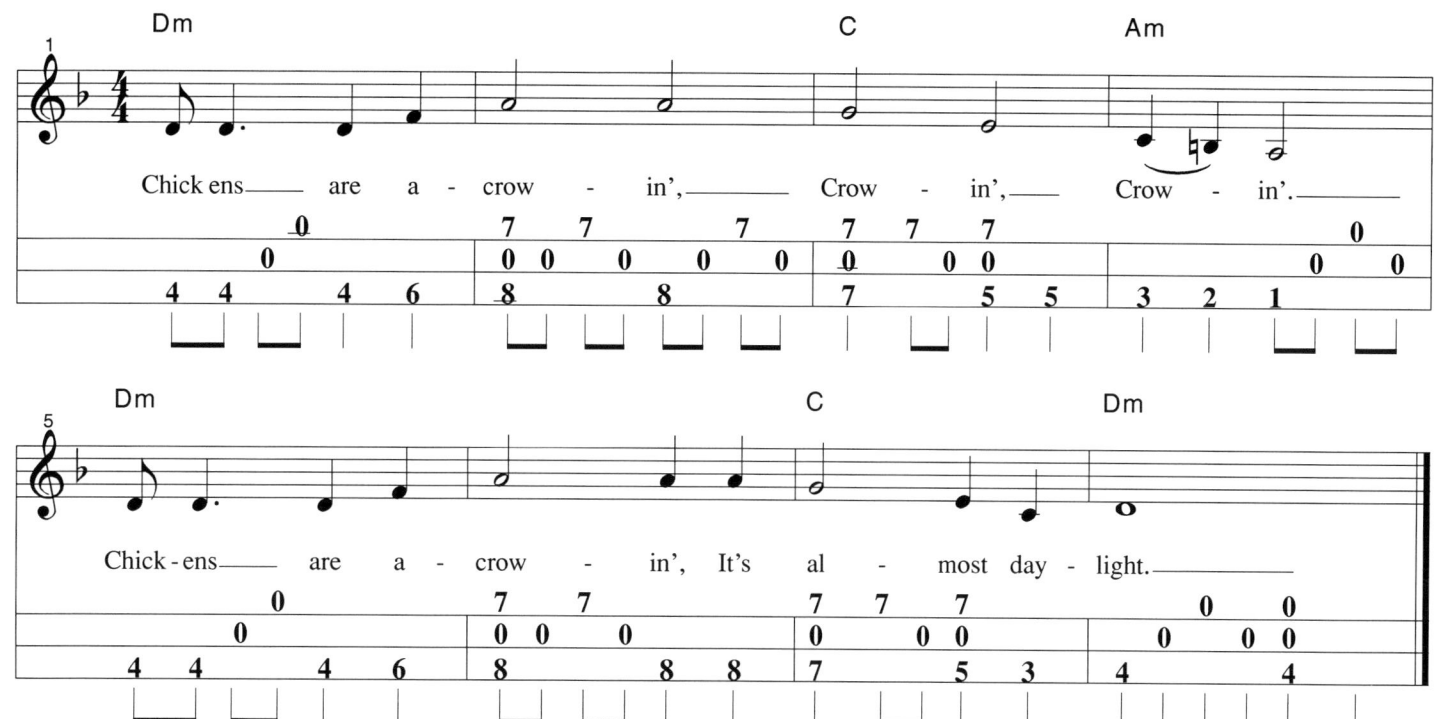

Chickens are a-crowin', crowin,' crowin.'
Chickens are a-crowin, it's almost daylight.

Momma's going to scold me, scold me, scold me,
Mamma's going to scold me for staying out all night.

Pappa, he'll uphold me, uphold me, uphold me,
Pappa, he'll uphold me, say I done just right.

I won't come home 'till morning, 'till morning, 'till morning,
I won't come home 'till morning, stay with the girls all night.

Chickens are a-crowin', crowin', crowin',
Chickens are a-crowin', it's almost daylight.

    This simple, haunting little tune is one the the most beautiful songs that entered the Sandal Shop. Ralph learned it from Allan Block. The song was collected by the English folklorist Cecil Sharp from Mr. Ben Findlay, Little Goose Creek, Kentucky, in 1917, and appears in Sharp's *English Folk Songs from the Southern Appalachians*.

The Brave Engineer

Tune D A A

Strum

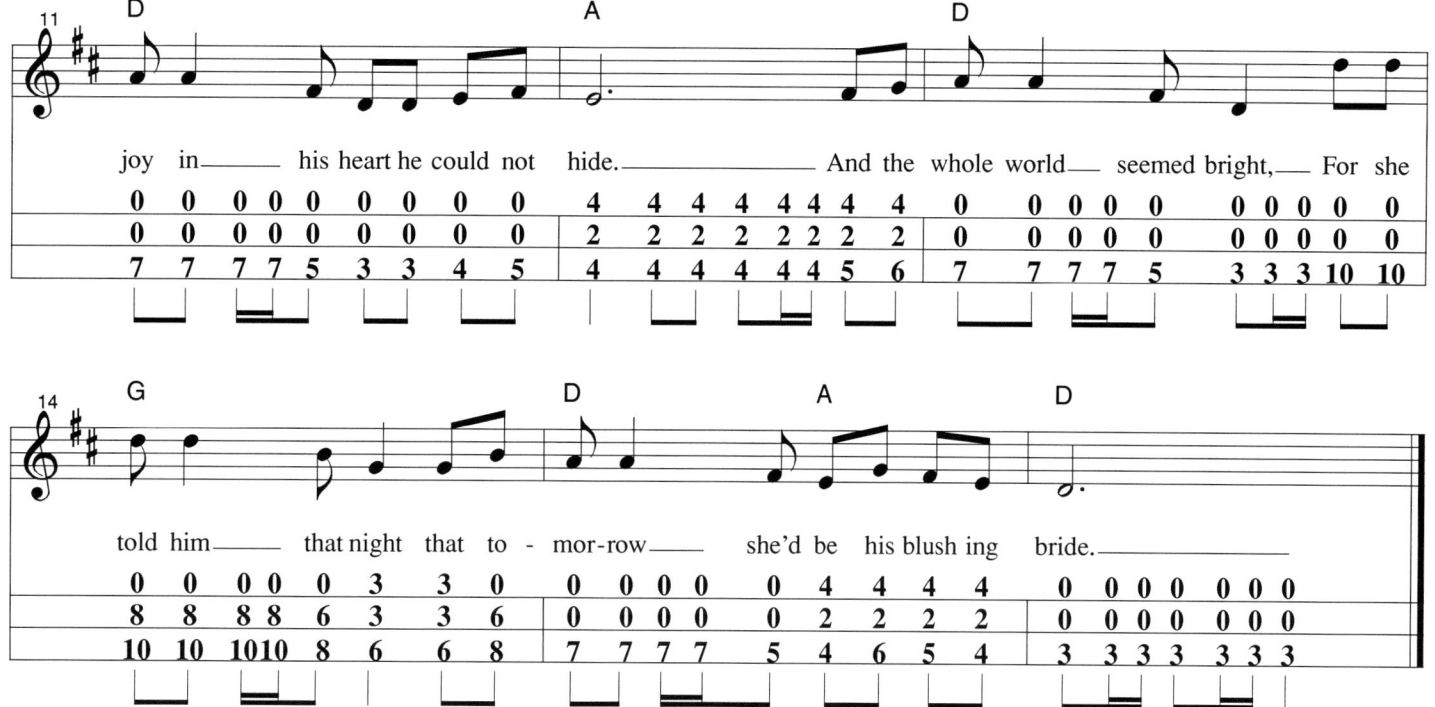

On a cold winter's night, not a star was in sight
And the north wind came howling down the line.
With his sweetheart so dear stood a brave engineer,
With his orders to pull old Number Nine.

With a tear in her eye she kissed him goodbye,
And the joy in his heart he could not hide.
And the whole world seemed bright for she told him that night
That tomorrow she'd be his blushing bride.

Oh, the wheels hummed a song as the train rolled along
And the black smoke came pouring from the stack.
And the headlight that gleamed seemed to brighten his dream
Of the morrow when he'd be coming back.

As he rounded the hill his brave heart stood still,
For a headlight was shining in his face.
And he uttered a prayer as he threw on the air
For he knew that he'd run his final race.

In the wreck he was found, lying there on the ground
And he asked them to lift his weary head;
As his life slowly went, this message he sent
To the girl who thought that she'd be wed.

There's a little white home that I built for our own
Where I thought we'd be happy by and by;
And I leave it to you, for I know you'll be true
Till we meet at that Golden Gate. Goodbye.

"The Brave Engineer" is on a 10-inch Folkways LP, *900 Miles and Other Railroad Songs*, sung by Cisco Houston with guitar, which was one of the best-loved of Ralph's Village records. It is an early Folkways release, bearing number FP13, that Ralph purchased in the Folklore Center in the late 50s. In addition to "The Brave Engineer" the record's title song, "900 Miles," is one of the most wonderful of all folk revival recordings.

The Brave Engineer

Tune D A D

Strum

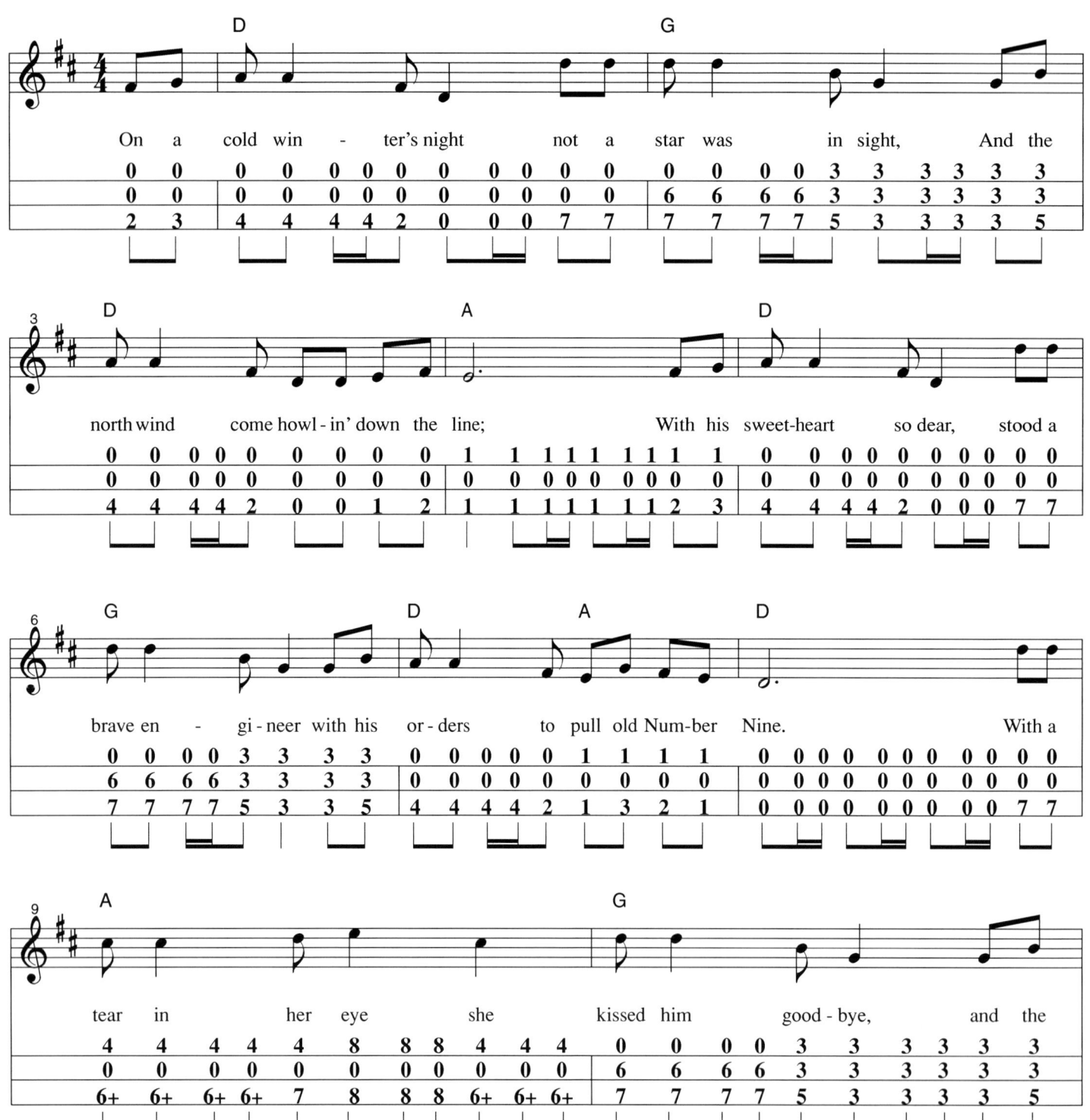

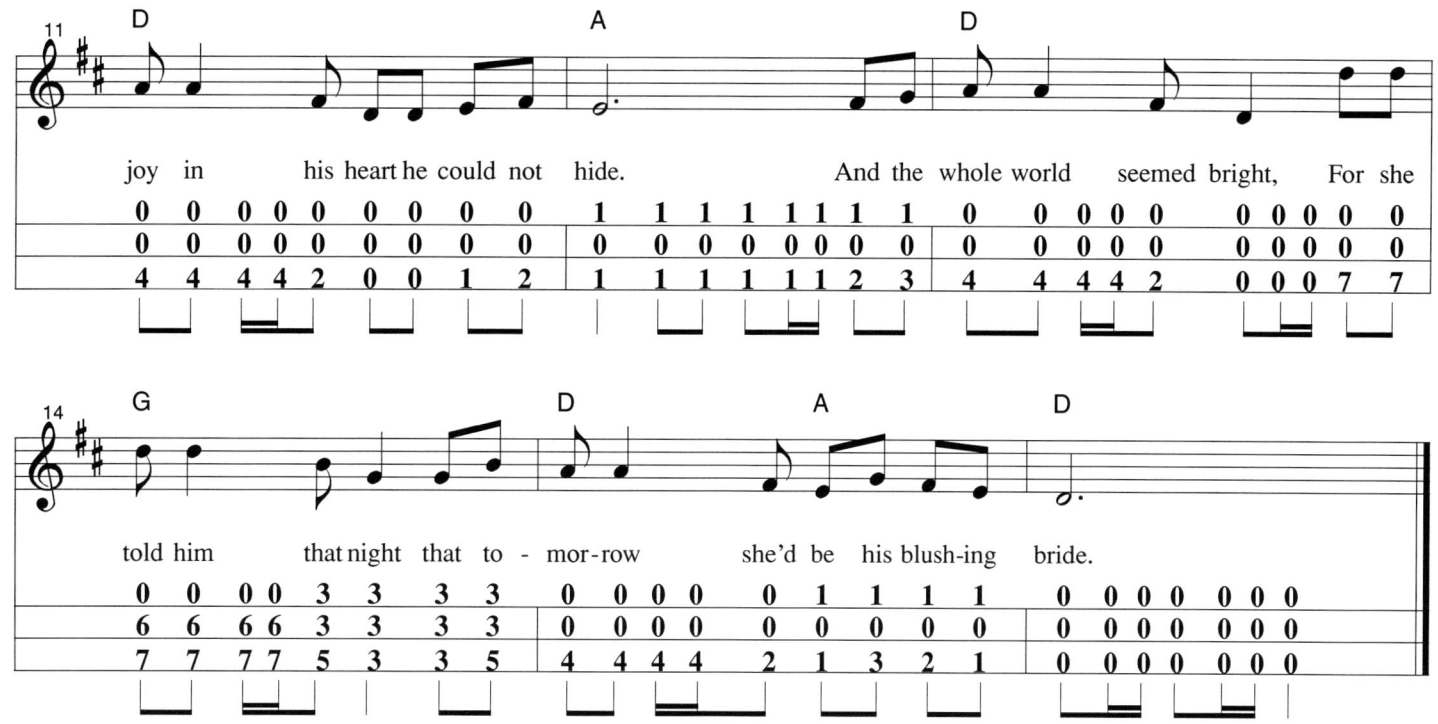

On a cold winter's night, not a star was in sight
And the north wind came howling down the line.
With his sweetheart so dear stood a brave engineer,
With his orders to pull old Number Nine.

With a tear in her eye she kissed him goodbye,
And the joy in his heart he could not hide.
And the whole world seemed bright for she told him that night
That tomorrow she'd be his blushing bride.

Oh, the wheels hummed a song as the train rolled along
And the black smoke came pouring from the stack.
And the headlight that gleamed seemed to brighten his dream
Of the morrow when he'd be coming back.

As he rounded the hill his brave heart stood still,
For a headlight was shining in his face.
And he uttered a prayer as he threw on the air
For he knew that he'd run his final race.

In the wreck he was found, lying there on the ground
And he asked them to lift his weary head;
As his life slowly went, this message he sent
To the girl who thought that she'd be wed.

There's a little white home that I built for our own
Where I thought we'd be happy by and by;
And I leave it to you, for I know you'll be true
Till we meet at that Golden Gate. Goodbye.

Ain't That Skippin' And a-Flyin'

Tune D A A
Strum

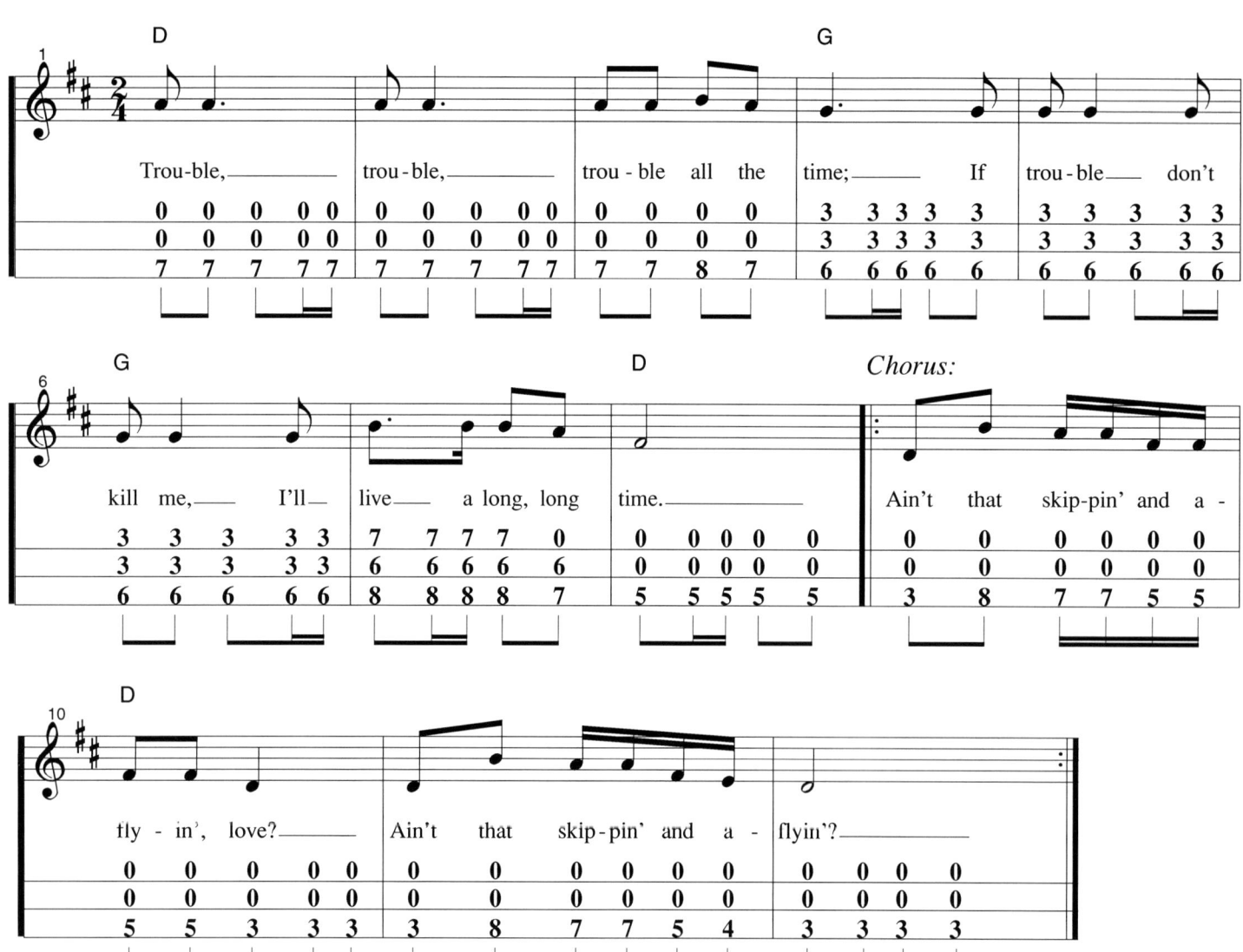

Art Rosenbaum, banjo player and field collector, brought this fine tune into the Sandal Shop. As Ralph recalls, the first three verses given here were sung by Art. He cannot recall the rest of Art's verses. However, a close variant of the song, entitled, "Ain't That Trouble in Mind," appears on a reissue in Ralph's Village record collection entitled, *The Original Bogtrotters, Recorded for the Library of Congress 1937-1942*, Biograph RC-6003. Verses 4 and 5 are from this recording. There is a sixth verse on the Bogtrotters recording, about dying and going to heaven, that Ralph can't make out. If anyone can decipher this verse or knows it, Ralph very much wants it!

Ain't That Skippin' And a-Flyin'

Tune D A D
Strum

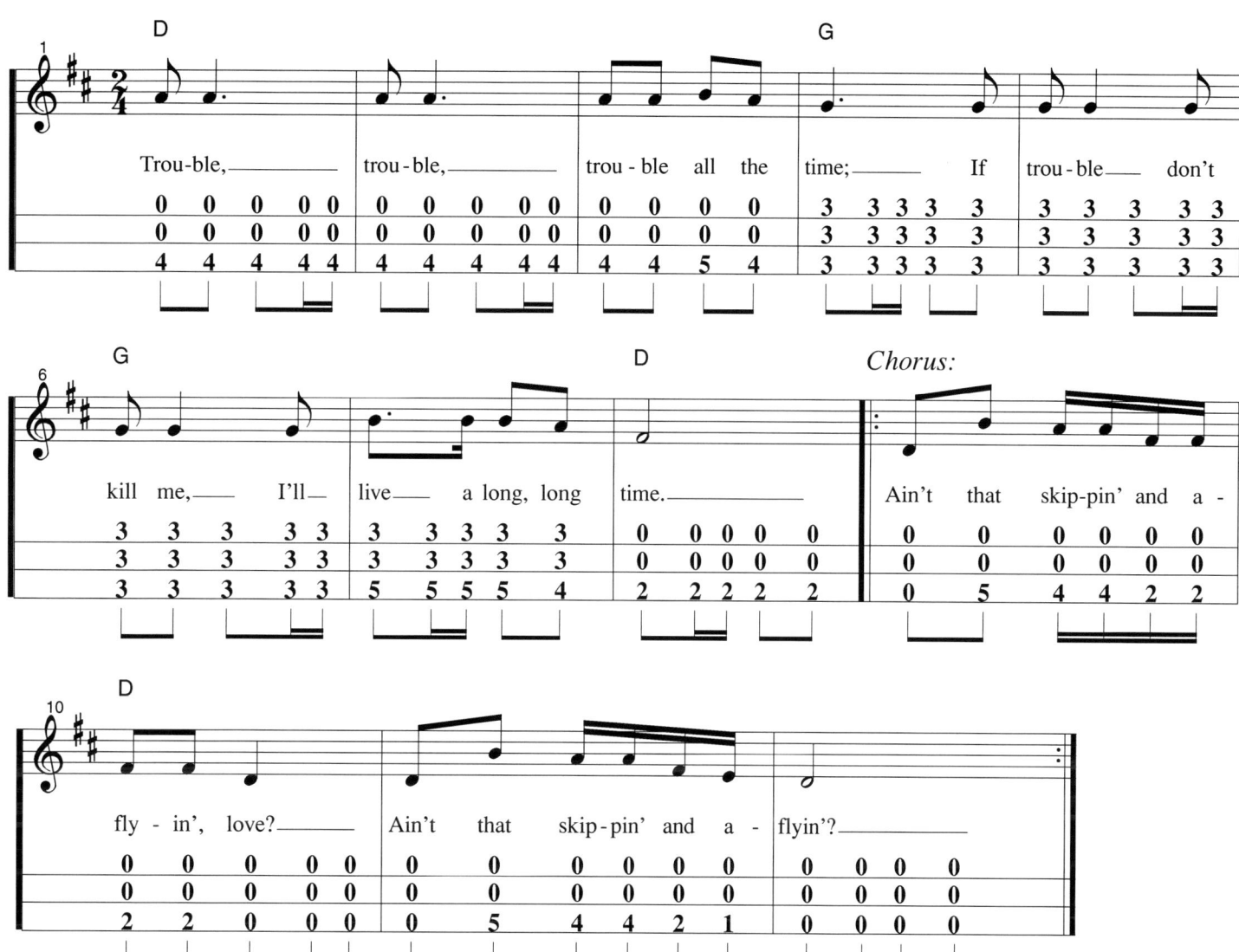

I went up on the mountain
To cut my sugar cane;
And every 'tarnal stalk I cut
I thought of Susan Jane.
Chorus:

Sometimes I've got money
Sometimes I've got none;
When I go on a drunken spree
My money's soon all gone.
Chorus:

My daddy told me to marry,
But not for love nor riches;
Marry a gal about six foot tall,
She can't wear my britches.
Chorus:

My mommy told me something,
My daddy told me more;
That if I married in this world
Be trouble at my door.
Chorus:

East Virginia

Tune D A A
Strum

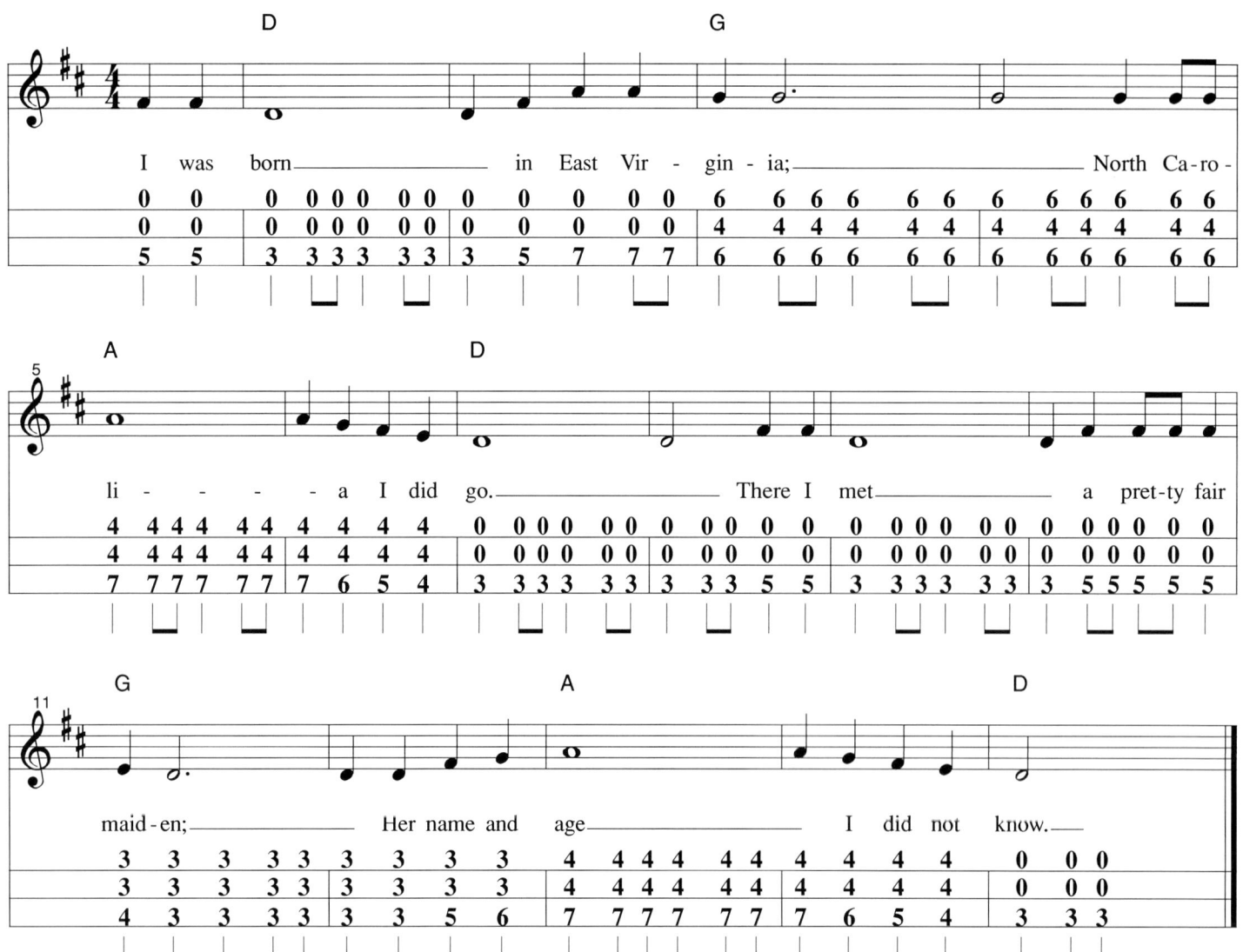

I was born in East Virginia
North Carolina I did go;
There I met a pretty fair maiden
Whose name and age I did not know.

Her hair was dark in color
Her cheeks were of a rosy red,
At my heart I loved her dearly
Many a tear for her I shed.

At my heart you are my darling
At my door you're welcome in,
At my gate I'll always greet you
Oh, if your heart I could only win.

I'd rather be in some dark holler
Where that sun don't never shine,
Than for you to be another man's darlin'
When I know that you should be mine.

I don't want your greenback dollar
I don't want your golden ring,
All I want is your heart, darling
Say you'll come to me again.

I was born in East Virginia
North Carolina I did go;
There I met a pretty fair maiden
Whose name and age I did not know.

    Ralph knew and sang four versions of "East Virginia" in the Village, one from traditional Virginia singer Harry West (see headnote to "Finger Ring"), one by the Carter Family, one by Jean Ritchie, and one put together by the New Lost City Ramblers. Ralph especially likes the tune of the Ramblers' version, which is given here, with verses as sung in the Sandal Shop.

East Virginia

Tune D A D
Strum

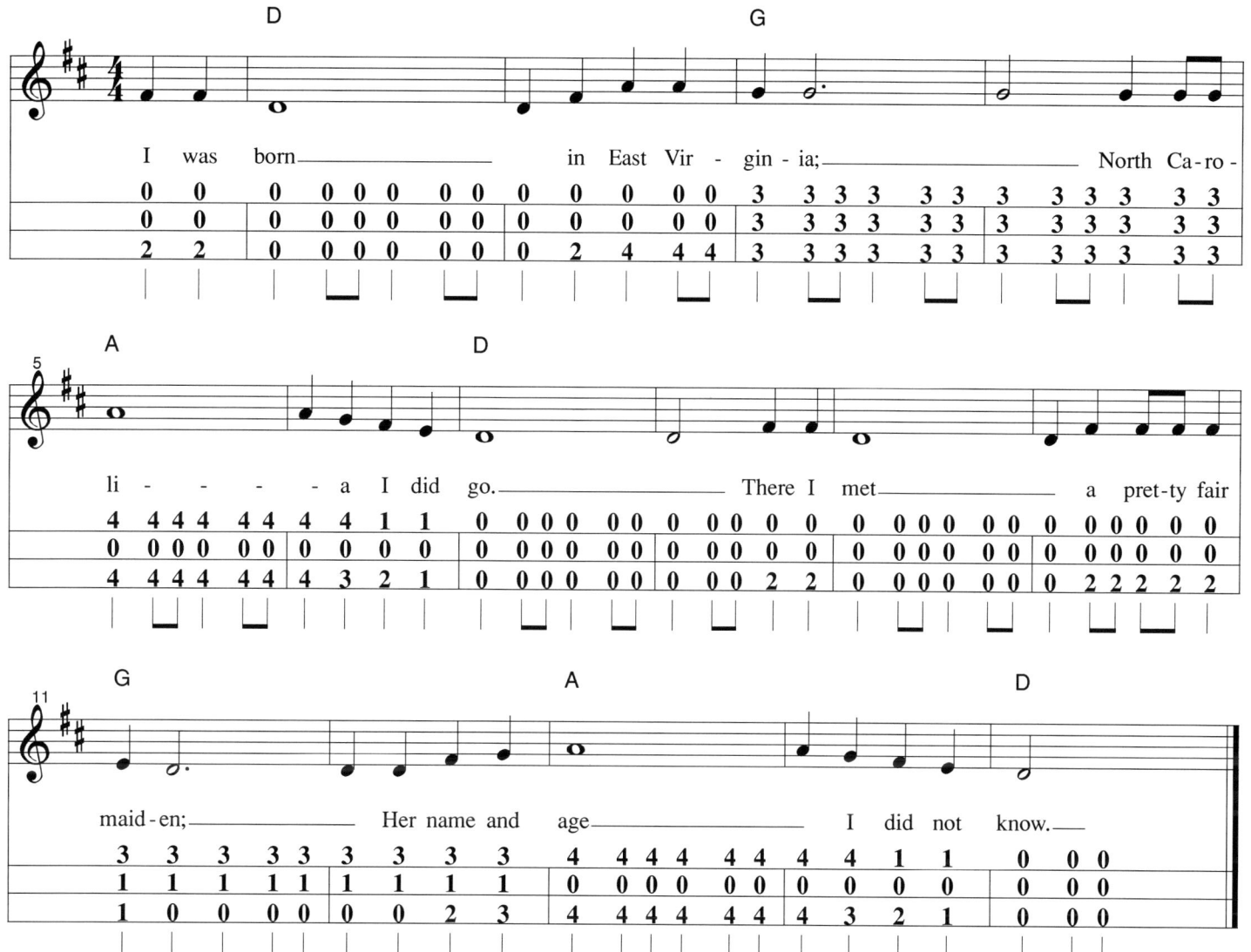

I was born in East Virginia
North Carolina I did go;
There I met a pretty fair maiden
Whose name and age I did not know.

Her hair was dark in color
Her cheeks were of a rosy red,
At my heart I loved her dearly
Many a tear for her I shed.

At my heart you are my darling
At my door you're welcome in,
At my gate I'll always greet you
Oh, if your heart I could only win.

I'd rather be in some dark holler
Where that sun don't never shine,
Than for you to be another man's darlin'
When I know that you should be mine.

I don't want your greenback dollar
I don't want your golden ring,
All I want is your heart, darling
Say you'll come to me again.

I was born in East Virginia
North Carolina I did go;
There I met a pretty fair maiden
Whose name and age I did not know.

Pretty Little Turtle Dove

Tune D A A
Fingerpick

76

Pretty Little Turtle Dove

    Ralph brought this song to the Village folk scene and the Sandal Shop. He learned it from the singing of Jerry Reed, brother of the early urban folksinger Susan Reed, when Susan was the featured performer at the Swarthmore College Folk Festival in 1948 and Jerry came along with her. Ralph does not know where Jerry learned his version. In 1968, County Records issued an LP entitled, *Old-Time Classics: A Collection of Mountain Banjo Songs & Tunes*, County 515. On this record, the traditional North Carolina banjo player Bascom Lamar Lunsford sings "Little Turtle Dove" in a 1920s recording. Lunsford's tune is a variant of the one learned from Jerry, but the two versions have only their first verse in common. Ralph used to enjoy playing Jerry's version in front of the fireplace at 4 Jones Street. (Maybe a pretty young lady was there, listening happily, who knows?) In either version, the song was and is surprisingly uncommon. The version here is Jerry's.

Pretty little turtle dove
Settin' in the pine,
Mournin' for his own true love
And why not me for mine, for mine?
Why not me for mine?

Up on the mountain the other day
A pretty little flower grew.
Never did I know 'til the other day
What love, oh love could do, could do,
What love, oh love could do.

Now she's gone and left me
Standin' in the rain,
Mourning for my own true love
's never going to come again, again,
's never going to come again.

If I had a scolding wife
Tell you sure as you're born,
I'd take her down to New Orleans
Swap her off for corn, for corn,
Swap her off for corn.

I am a country boy,
Money I've got none;
Still there's silver in the stars,
Gold in the morning sun, sun,
Gold in the morning sun.

Pretty Little Turtle Dove

Tune D A D
Fingerpick

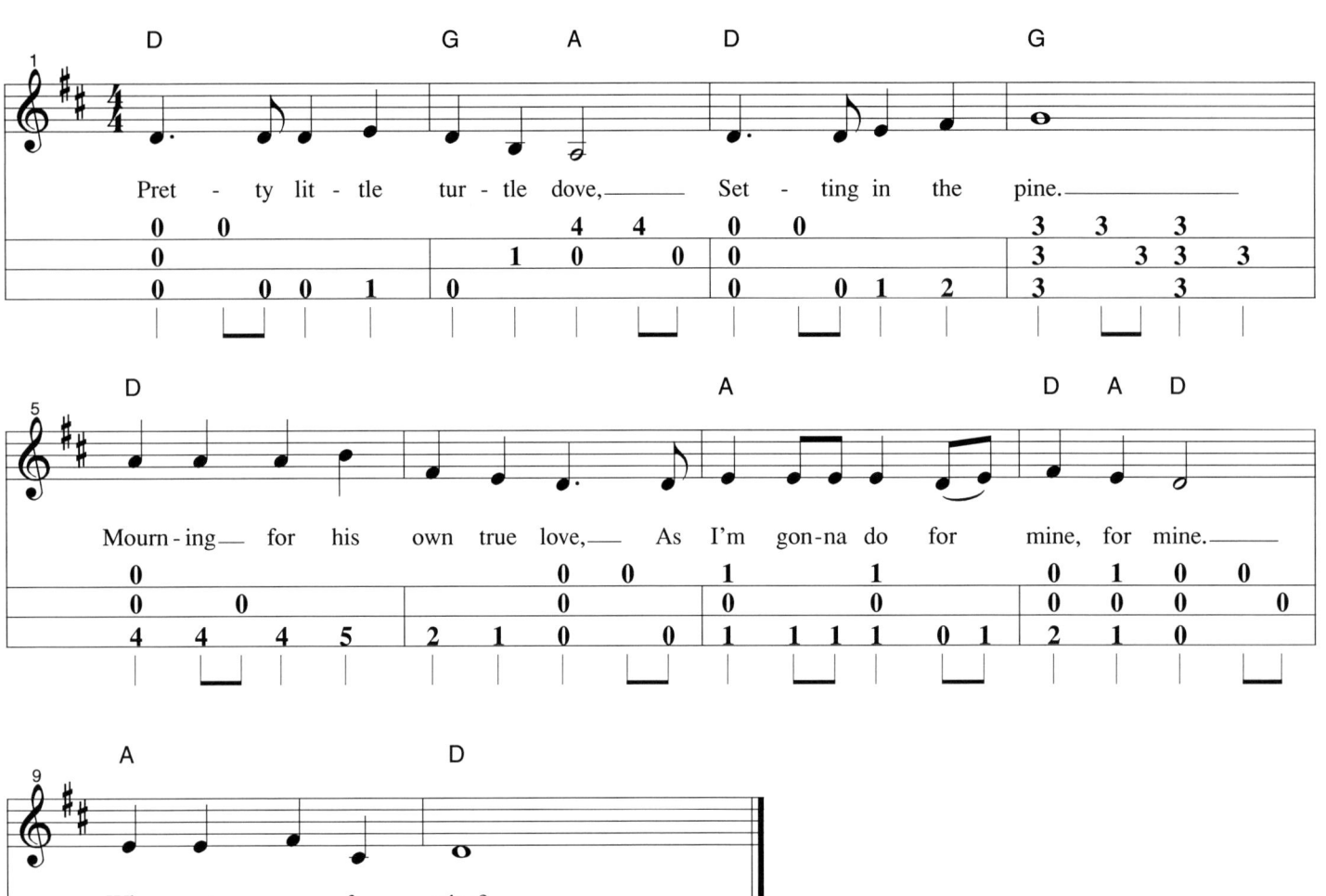

Up on the mountain the other day
A pretty little flower grew.
Never did I know 'til the other day
What love, oh love could do, could do,
What love, oh love could do.

Now she's gone and left me
Standin' in the rain,
Mourning for my own true love
's never going to come again, again,
's never going to come again.

If I had a scolding wife
Tell you sure as you're born,
I'd take her down to New Orleans
Swap her off for corn, for corn,
Swap her off for corn.

I am a country boy,
Money I've got none;
Still there's silver in the stars,
Gold in the morning sun, sun,
Gold in the morning sun.

Hop High Ladies

Tune D A A
Strum

Hop High Ladies

"Hop High Ladies" consists of words that have been put to an old fiddle tune called "Miss MacLeod's Reel." A rollicking version was recorded by Uncle Dave Macon in the 1920s. It appears in the *New Lost City Ramblers Songbook*, but without the final verse given here, which was always sung in the Sandal Shop. Ralph does not know its source. The line that is repeated three times in the chorus is sometimes sung as "Hop high ladies, three in a row."

Have you ever been to meeting Uncle Joe, Uncle Joe?
Have you ever been to meeting, Uncle Joe?
Have you ever been to meeting, Uncle Joe, Uncle Joe?
Well, I don't mind the weather so the wind don't blow.

Chorus:
Hop high ladies, for the cake's all dough
Hop high ladies, for the cake's all dough
Hop high ladies, for the cake's all dough
How I ever get the time, Lord I never will know.

Will your horse carry double, Uncle Joe, Jucle Joe?
Will your horse carry double, Uncle Joe?
Will your horse carry double, Uncle Joe, Uncle Joe?
Well, I don't mind the weather so the wind don't blow.

Is your horse a single footer, Uncle Joe, Uncle Joe?
Is your horse a single footer, Uncle Joe?
Is your horse a single footer, Uncle Joe, Uncle Joe?
Well, I don't mind the weather so the wind don't blow.

How do you like the ladies, Uncle Joe, Uncle Joe?
How do you like the ladies, Uncle Joe?
How do you like the ladies, Uncle Joe, Uncle Joe?
Well, I don't mind the weather so the wind don't blow.

Hop High Ladies

Tune D A D
Strum

Goin' Across The Sea

Tune D A A
Strum

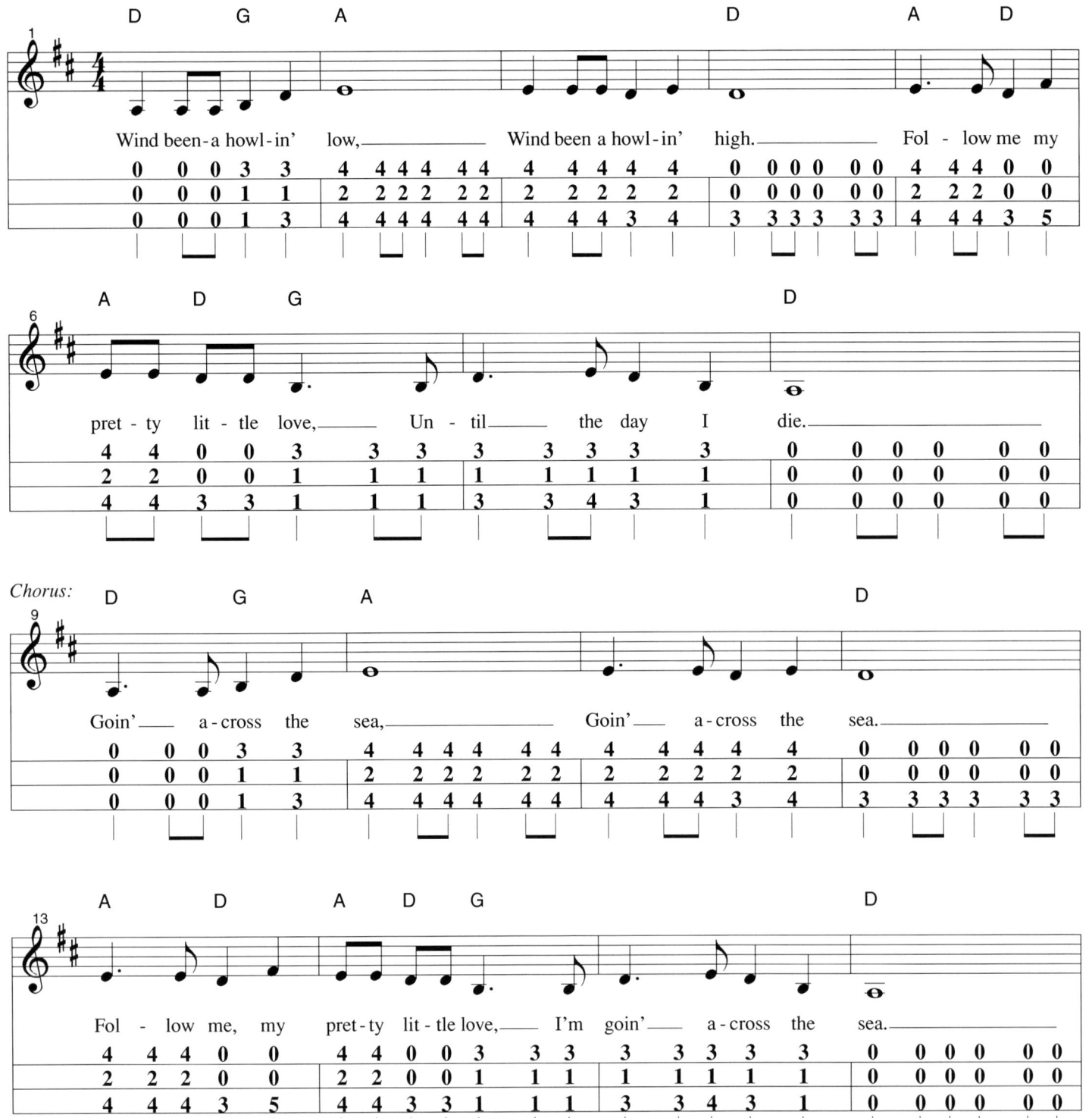

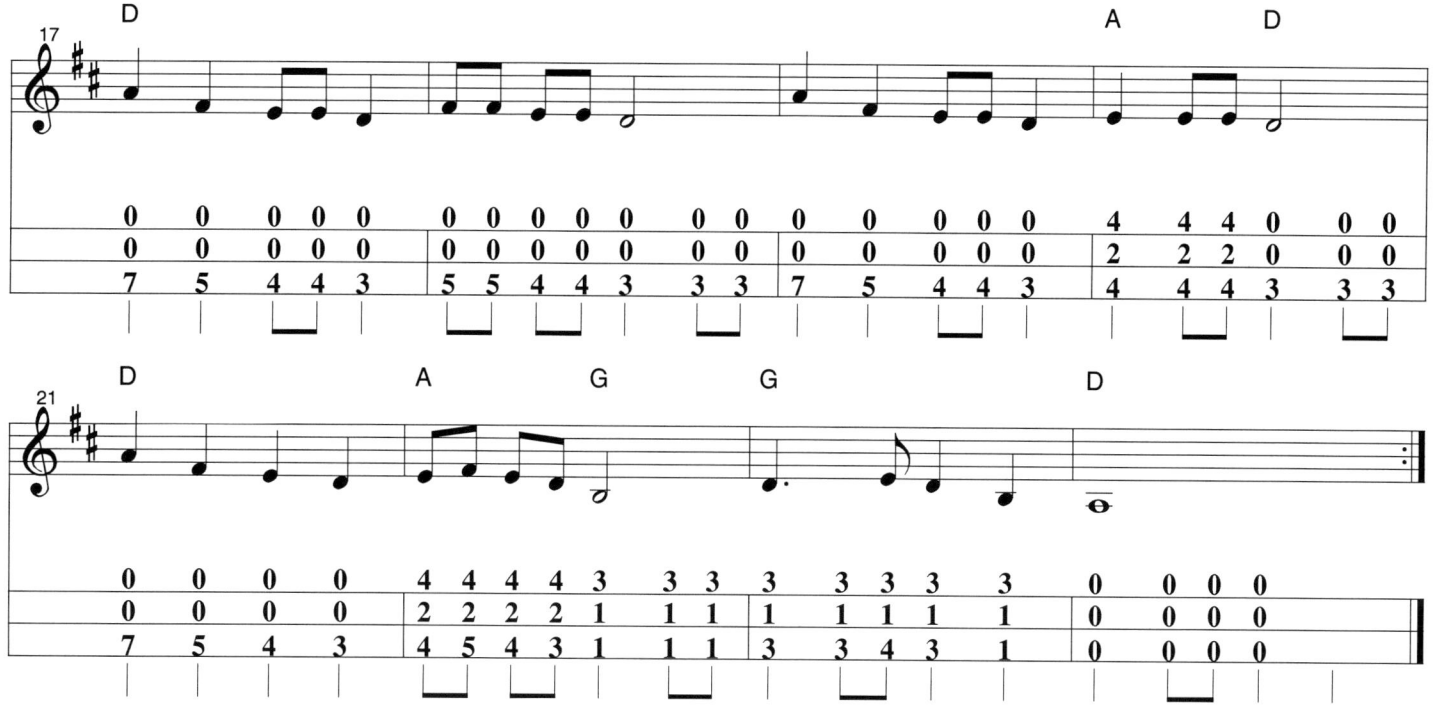

Playing Note: Because the singing portion of this song has a limited range clustering around the first note of the scale, you may wish to raise the pitch of your strings from DAA to EBB to make the singing a bit easier.

Chorus:
Goin' across the sea
Goin' across the sea.
Follow me, my pretty little love,
I'm goin' across the sea.

Wind been a-howlin' low,
Wind been a-howlin' high.
Follow me, my pretty little love,
Until the day I die.

Can't you change a nickel?
Can't you change a dime?
Can't you come to Tennessee
And change your name to mine?

Higher up the cherry tree
Riper grow the cherries;
More you hug and kiss the girls
Sooner you will marry.

Rose as red a cherry,
Cherry red as a plum.
My pretty little girl is a-callin' me
I know I'm bound to come.

Way across the sea,
Way across the sea.
Hear my true love whistlin'
Way across the sea.

This song appears on a County Records reissue, entitled, *Uncle Dave Macon: Early Recordings*, County 52, an adored record in Ralph's 60s collection. Playing it after the lapse of some thirty years, he found that the typed set of words in his old three-ring notebook is mostly different from those sung by Uncle Dave on this record. Ralph thinks that Art Rosenbaum is the source. Under any circumstances, here it is: Uncle Dave's tune and a fine set of traditional words from Art—or somebody!

Roll On The Ground

Tune D A A
Strum

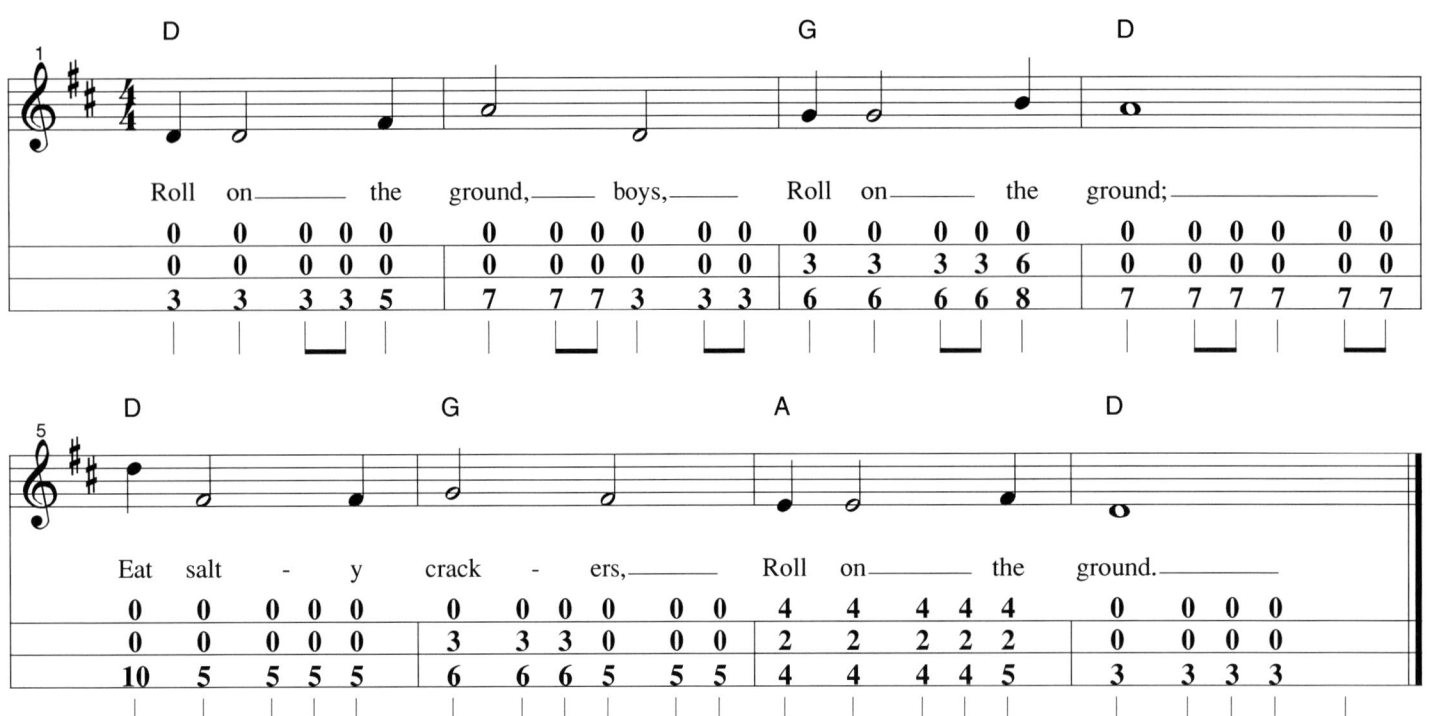

Work on the railroad,
Sleep on the ground;
Eat salty crackers,
The wind blows 'em around.

Work on the railroad,
Three cents a day;
Eat salty crackers,
Sleep in the hay.

Big ball in Nashville,
Big ball in town;
Big ball in Nashville,
Let's dance around.

You've got a nickel,
I've got a dime;
Let's go to town, babe,
We'll have a time.

Chorus:
Roll on the ground, boys,
Roll on the ground;
Eat salty crackers,
Roll on the ground.

This song, learned from Allan Block, was a staple of the Saturday afternoon music sessions in the Sandal Shop. Allan learned it from a 1939 recording by a banjo player named Thaddeus P. Willingham, who was an engineer on the Southern Pacific Railroad. Willingham's recording appears on the Library of Congress record AAFSL2, *Anglo-American Shanties, Lyric Songs, Dance Tunes and Spirituals*. Ralph plays it on the recording *Allan Block and Ralph Lee Smith*.

Roll On The Ground

Tune D A D
Strum

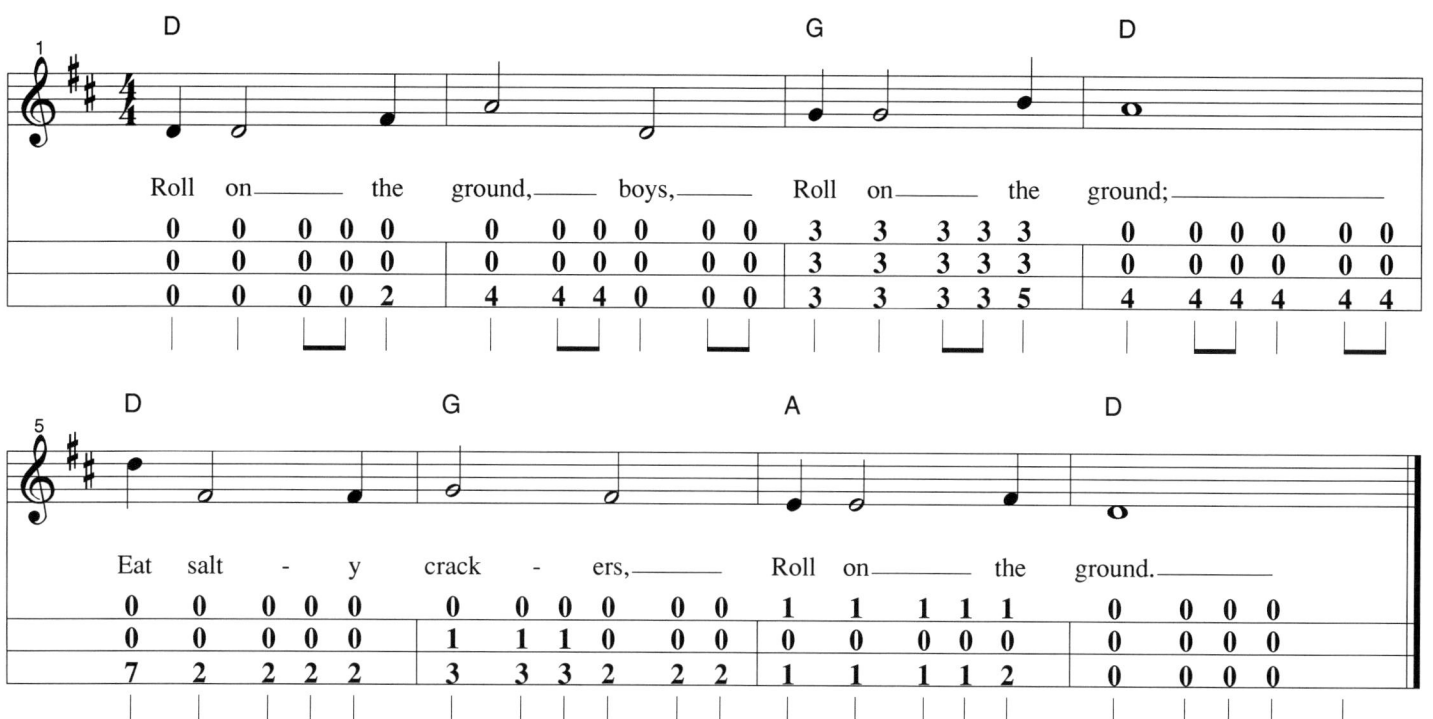

Work on the railroad,
Sleep on the ground;
Eat salty crackers,
The wind blows 'em around.

Work on the railroad,
Three cents a day;
Eat salty crackers,
Sleep in the hay.

Big ball in Nashville,
Big ball in town;
Big ball in Nashville,
Let's dance around.

You've got a nickel,
I've got a dime;
Let's go to town, babe,
We'll have a time.

Chorus:
Roll on the ground, boys,
Roll on the ground;
Eat salty crackers,
Roll on the ground.

Likes Likker Better Than Me

Tune D A A
Strum

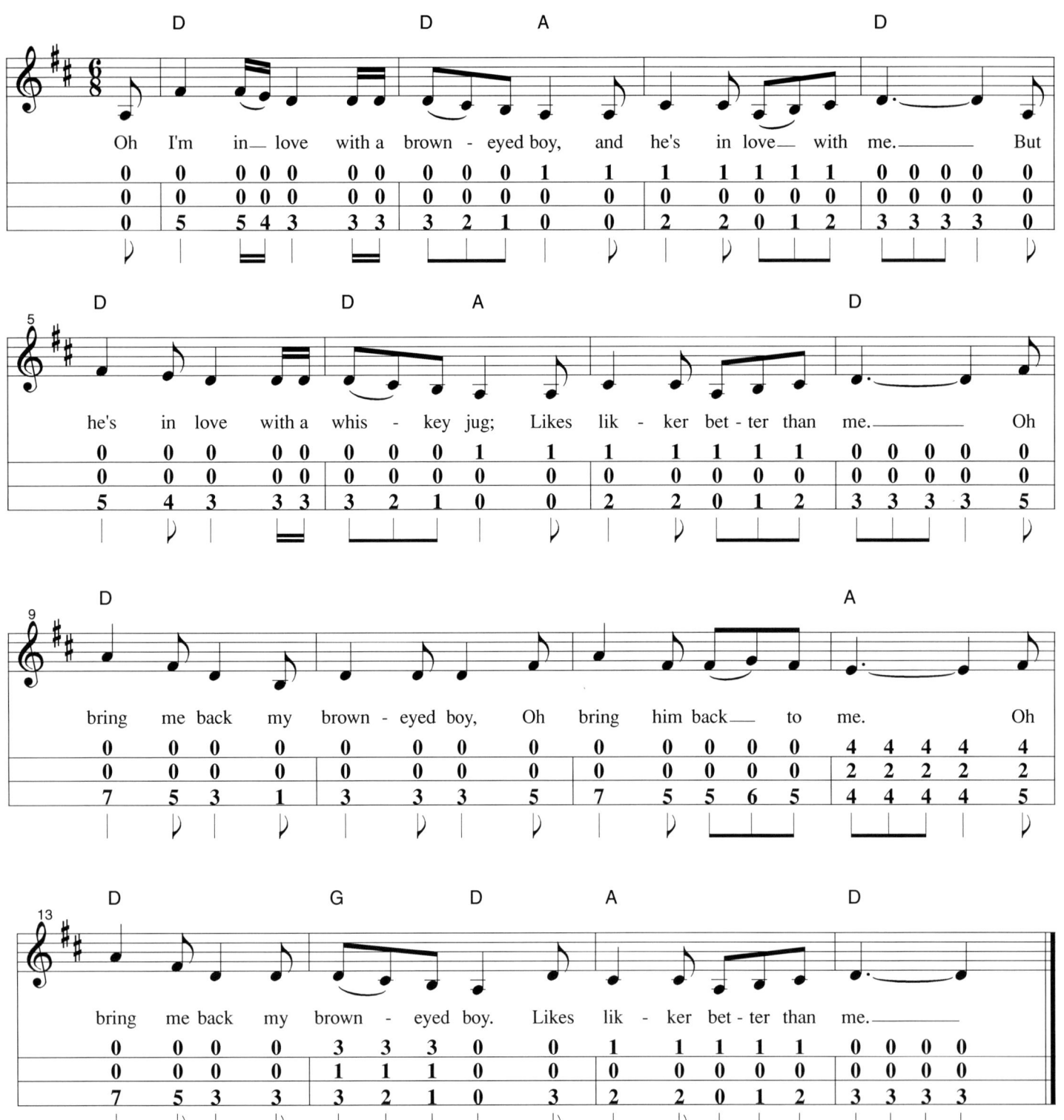

Likes Likker Better Than Me

This song was a guaranteed crowd-pleaser at the Sandal Shop. Ralph remembers singing it at the top of his lungs, in exaggerated lachrymose tones, to make sure that everyone who was standing outside the Shop on summer afternoons could hear it! He sometimes got a nice hand! Originally, this was a temperance song, and was not intended to be funny. It has shared the fate of some of the songs of Blind Alfred Reed that warn girls against worldly boys, that they now inspire more smiles than resolutions to follow the straight and narrow.

Oh, I'm in love with a brown-eyed boy
And he's in love with me.
But he's in love with a whiskey jug,
Likes likker better than me.

Chorus:
Oh, bring me back my brown-eyed boy,
Bring him back to me.
Bring me back my brown-eyed boy,
Likes likker better than me.

Last night he came to see me,
Last night he smiled on me.
But tonight he smiles on a whiskey jug,
Likes likker better than me.

Sometimes I think that I'll marry him,
For I love him dearer than life.
But oh, it's all so hard to bear,
As a whiskey drinker's wife.

1969 Indian Neck Folk Festival
Ralph playing with Lorraine Lee Hammond at the Indian Neck Folk Festival, 1969. Photo by Photo-Sound Associates. Used with permission.

Likes Likker Better Than Me

Tune D A D
Strum

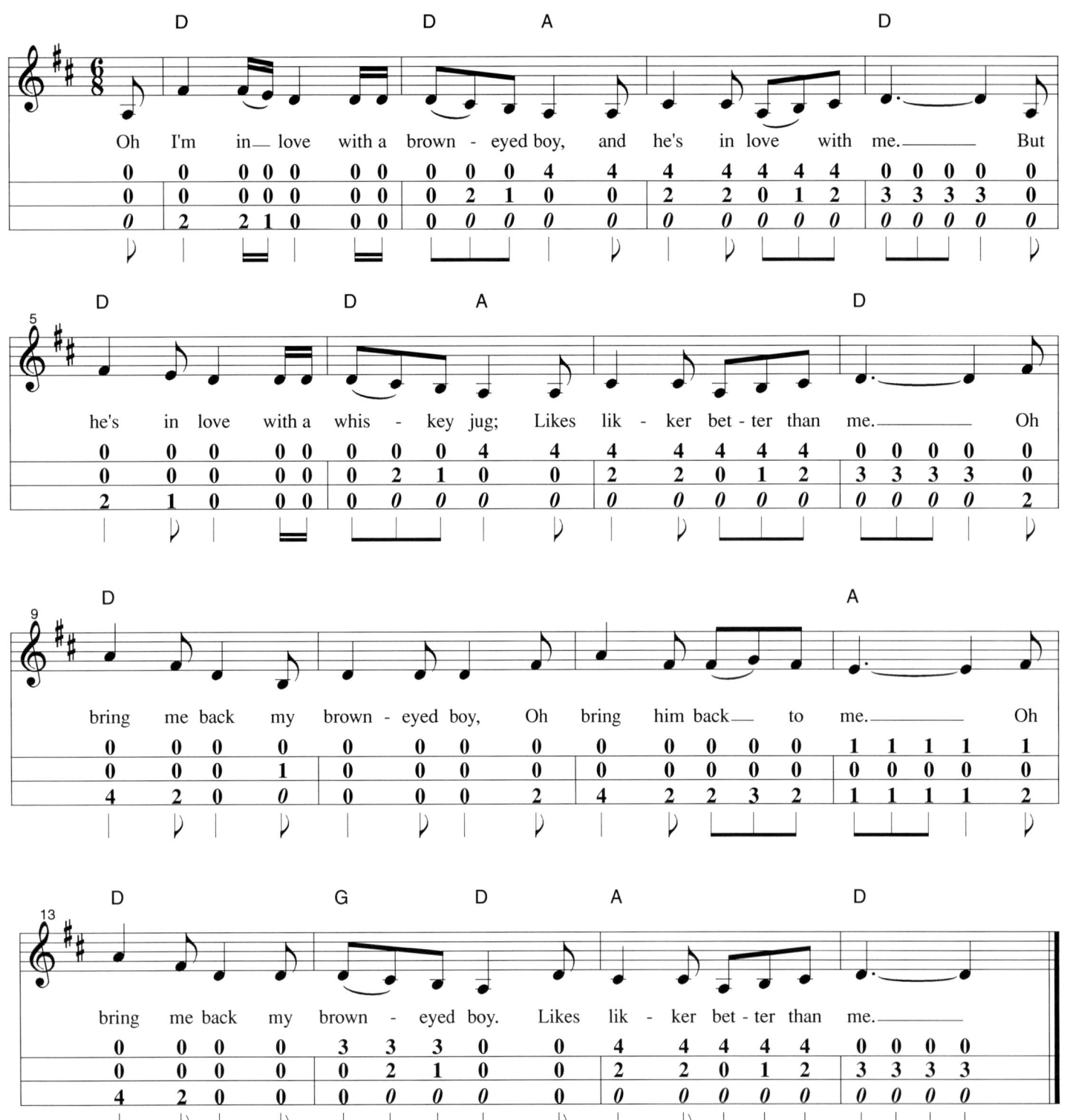

Italic tablature numbers: Melody is on the middle string. Strum all of the strings, but emphasize the middle string.

Georgia Railroad

Tune D A A
Strum

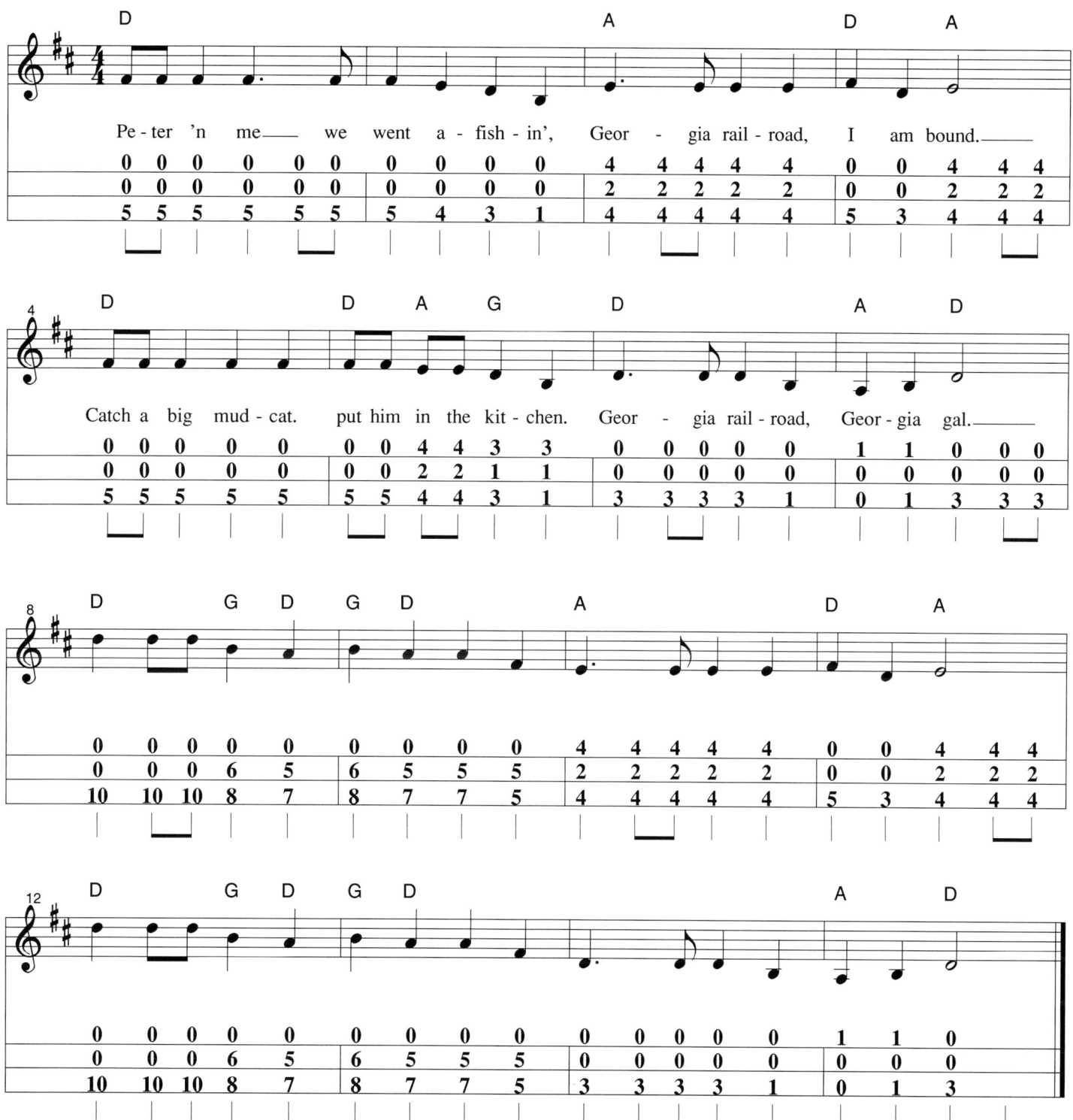

89

Georgia Railroad

Ralph learned this song from Richard Blaustein in the Sandal Shop. It is played on *Allan Block and Ralph Lee Smith*, with Allan on fiddle and voice, Rob on guitar, and Ralph on harmonica. Traditional sources include a recording by Gid Tanner and the Skillet Lickers, with the title, "Peter Went a-Fishing." In the Sandal Shop, where folks joined enthusiastically together in singing and playing the song, no one played the second part the same way. As given here, it is what Ralph remembers, more or less!

Peter and me, we went a'fishing,
Georgia railroad, I am bound.
Catch a big mudcat, put him in the kitchen
Georgia railroad, Georgia gal.

Goin' down the road, the road's mighty muddy,
Georgia railroad, I am bound.
So durned drunk I can't stand steady,
Georgia railroad, Georgia gal.

Cow and sheep's put to pasture,
Georgia railroad I am bound.
Cow said, "Sheep can't you go any faster?"
Georgia railroad, Georgia gal.

(Repeat first verse)

Georgia Railroad

Tune D A D
Strum

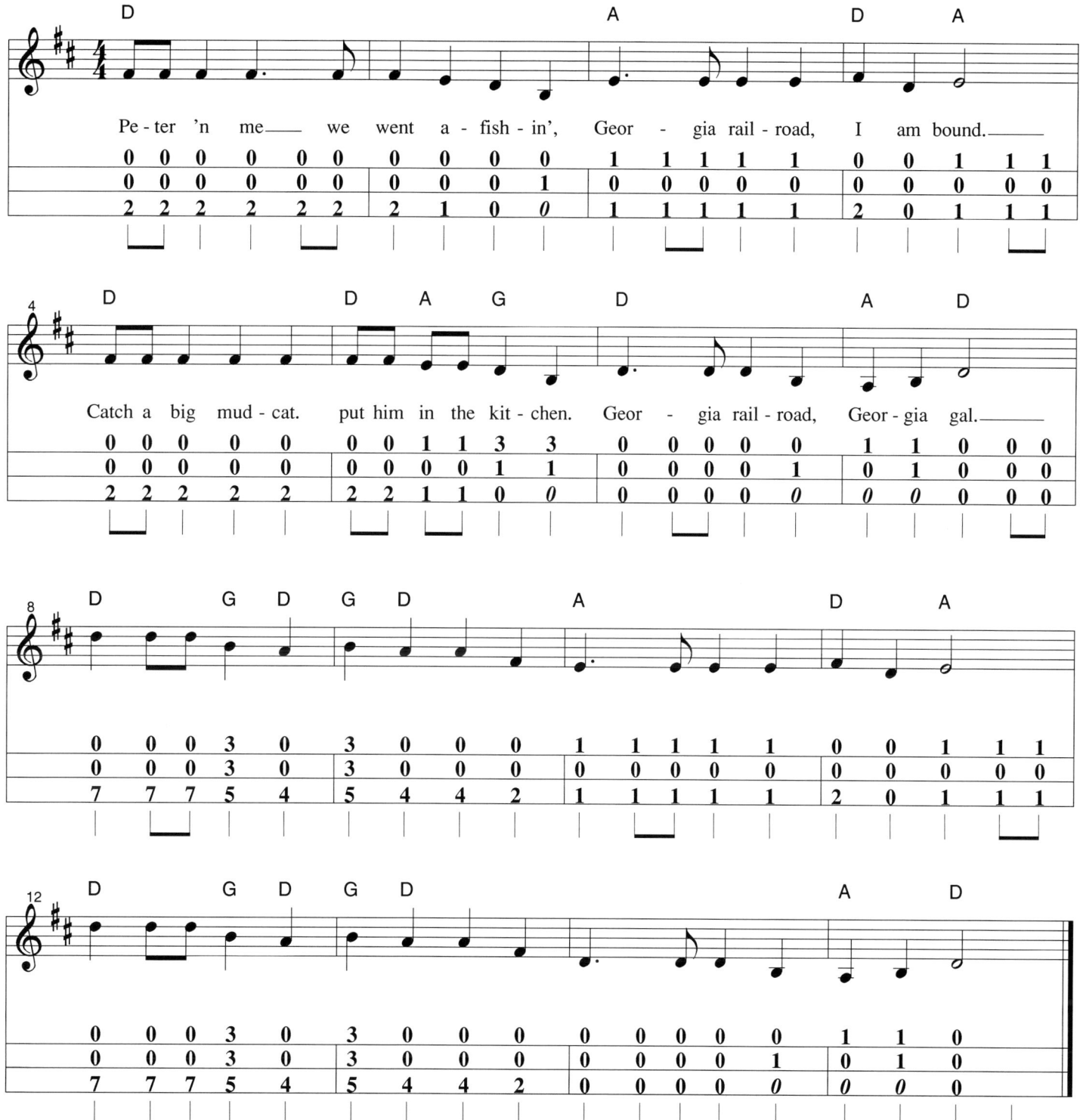

Italic tablature numbers: Melody is on the middle string. Strum all of the strings, but emphasize the middle string.

Who's Going To Shoe Your Pretty Little Foot?

Tune D A A
Fingerpick

Who's Going To Shoe Your Pretty Little Foot?

Ralph picks and sings this song on his Jean Ritchie dulcimer on the record *Allan Block & Ralph Lee Smith*. He does not recall where he learned the tune. The words are cobbled together from four sources. The first two verses, which originally came from the British ballad "The Lass Of Roch Royal," appear in numerous American folksongs. He learned the third verse from Sandy Rainey Brown, a kind and lovely young person who arrived in the Village from Atlanta sometime in the 1960s. (Hello there, Sandy, wherever you are!) Ralph doesn't remember where the fourth verse came from. He borrowed the final two verses from the song "Good Morning, Mister Railroad Man." The result is a good example of the Sandal Shop folk process!

Who's going to shoe your pretty little foot?
Who's going to glove your hand?
Who's going to kiss your red ruby lips?
Who's going to be your man?

Papa's going to shoe my pretty little foot,
Mama's going to glove my hand;
Sister's going to kiss my red ruby lips,
I don't need no man.

The longest train I ever did see
Went down that Georgia line:
The engine it went by at six,
Caboose went by at nine.

The longest train I ever did see
Was a hundred coaches long;
The only girl I ever did love
Was on that train and gone.

I sat down at a gambling game
I couldn't play my hand,
Thinking about that girl I love
Gone away with another man.

Gone away with another man,
Gone away with another man;
Thinking about that girl I love
Gone away with another man.

The following four verses are from "The Lass Of Lochroyan," collected from Scottish oral tradition by the novelist Sir Walter Scott and published by him in his great work *Minstrelsy Of The Scottish Border*, issued in three volumes in 1802 and 1803.

O wha will shoe my bonny foot?
And wha will glove my hand?
And wha will lace my middle jimp
Wi' a lang, lang linen band?

O wha will kame my yellow hair,
With a new-made silver kame?
And wha will father my young son,
Till Lord Gregory come hame?

Thy father will shoe thy bonny foot,
Thy mother will glove thy hand,
Thy sister will lace thy middle jimp
Till Lord Gregory come to land.

Thy brother will kame thy yellow hair
With a new-made silver kame,
And God will be thy bairn's father
Till Lord Gregory come hame.

Who's Going To Shoe Your Pretty Little Foot?

Tune D A D
Fingerpick

Additional verses on previous page.

POSTSCRIPT

"A TIME OF JOY FROM OUR YOUTH"
By Eric Nagler

Eric Nagler, who played banjo in both Washington Square and the Sandal Shop in the 60s (See Page 23), now lives in Canada. When he returned home after attending the Third Annual Bluegrass and Old Timey Reunion in Washington Square on September 16, 2007 (See Page 39), he published the following in his local community newspaper. It is reprinted here with his permission.

Reunion

The Sun smiled warmly on the cluster of musicians, surrounded by a circle of excited spectators tapping their toes to a breakneck rendition of "Roll in My Sweet Baby's Arms". They didn't need to know each other to play beautifully and flawlessly, laying out or coming in when called upon and after each verse joining in the chorus in perfect harmony. They all knew their parts because they'd all heard The Bluegrass Boys sing and pick it. Maybe they'd sat like I did as a kid, ear to the record player for hours, listening over and over to the licks, the riffs, the nuances until we could play it just like Monroe, or Scruggs, or Watson, or any of those we chose as gurus of our instrument.

When the rat-a-tat-tat of the fiddle signaled the end of the song they all burst into laughter because it was sooo good, so clean. We laughed because for those of us who remembered, the thrill of the sixties rattled our bones and the common thread of this music called us back here forty years later to the Washington Square Third Annual Bluegrass and Old Timey Reunion.

There were a hundred, maybe more of us, laughing, chatting, schmoozing in the shadow of the Washington Square Arch, heading off in little groups of threes and fours to find a relatively quiet bench to recall tunes we'd shown each other decades ago. Some of us are lucky to still live near enough to play together. Others, like me, hopped a plane to be here to re-excite that spark and feed the musical flame that burns still in our hearts.

We laughed when we looked at each others' name tags and said, "My God! Nagler! Is that you?" We laughed when someone approached, wrinkled, bearded and bald, and showed us a picture of us playing together during some ancient summer of love, apple-cheeked faces filled with the exuberant glee of youth. We laughed when we recalled that party, or that girl, or that fateful evening after a concert when everyone decided to form a group and became famous for fifteen minutes.

The Square on a Sunday is a noisy place, with drummers, street actors, jugglers and clowns gathering audiences on the fly. But it is big enough to accommodate us all, and we certainly stood out, with our grey beards and Gibson banjos, joy shining through our wrinkles.

I was stopped by a young couple with wide eyes who asked what was going on, this odd party of high folk where music was the only cocktail served. I explained this was what we did as kids in the sixties, that the Internet had connected us again, and that now we come together one Sunday at the end of summer to relive a time of joy from our youth. And I told them I hoped when they were my age they had something like this to return to.